RAINMAKING

RAINMAKING

ROBERT MILLER

Printed in the United States of America

ISBN 978-0-9975887-1-2

CUATRO CORP.
IRVINE. CALIFORNIA

For Alicia and Ali

**Part of you pours out of me
In these lines from time to time**

— A Case of You — Joni Mitchell
Joni Mitchell (1971)

Contents

rain·mak·ing

the process of impacting the world through
the power of emotions
and the magic of storytelling

Foreword

You say you want to be a leader
But you can't seem to make up your mind
I think you better close it
And let me guide you to the purple rain

— *Purple Rain* — Prince
Prince (1983)

I met Robert Miller on my campaign trail.
He remembered me standing at different supermarkets in Irvine, asking for votes from the grocery shoppers. I came across hundreds, if not thousands, of people at the exit doors of supermarkets, at the door steps of their homes, and at hundreds of events that I attend throughout the community. I have met and forgotten thousands of them over the past eighteen years of my public life. Among them, Robert Miller was unique and unforgettable. He has written *Rainmaking* and has invited me to write this important Foreword.

In his Preface, Robert says "the World of Rainmaking . . . where you'll use the power of emotions and the magic of storytelling to achieve everything your heart desires." That is a powerful statement. Fast reading through his book draft, I find that Robert is presenting a full array of wisdom, with many quotes from wise and successful people. Each of them requires a deep meditation to digest into your blood stream to make it yours — only then will you become a "rainmaker." One definition of the role of the rainmaker is finding "a dormant business problem and then create a vision of what life could be if that problem were solved."

Robert must have regarded me as a rainmaker after watching from afar. As a politician, I am always exposed to the public view, regardless of my wishes. Many people behave as if they don't know me even if they do know me after eighteen years of rainmaking effort of my own in the public service and in the public view. Robert stepped out to tell me that he saw what I've been doing. He thinks I am a rainmaker, qualified to write a few words in this Foreword. I wish I had read his book eighteen years ago — I would be a better rainmaker today!

Steven S. Choi, Ph.D.
Member of the California State Assembly

Preface

Noah Curry: **We don't believe in rainmakers.**
Bill Starbuck: **What DO you believe in mistah? Dyin' cattle?**

— Noah Curry (Lloyd Bridges)
Bill Starbuck (Burt Lancaster)
The Rainmaker (1956)

Welcome to the wonderful world of Rainmaking. Like me, you want to make an impact on the world; maybe you have dreamed of doing something for a long time but haven't slowed down long enough to get started. By now, you realize that it's a fantastic time to be alive, and you're READY! Hopefully, you know your WHY. *Rainmaking* is going to help you with your what, how, and when.

Rainmaking is not about manipulative selling. It's not about putting a name badge on and working the room. It's not about passing out business cards or even about collecting them. It's not about continually reciting a canned elevator pitch or 30-second commercial, or being a trained monkey. *Rainmaking* is about connecting with people by investing the time to feel what they are feeling. It's about sincerely empathizing with them and using stories to transport them emotionally through time and space toward the realization of their dreams.

Reading this book will be an adventure. You are about to follow the Yellow Brick Road, fall down the Rabbit Hole, fly to Never-never Land, pass through the gates of Fantasyland, enter the Twilight Zone, and arrive at the World of *Rainmaking* — where you'll use the power of emotions and the magic of storytelling to achieve everything your heart desires. Close your eyes and wish upon a star . . . here we go!

Do you want to sell sugar water the rest of your life, or do you want to come with me and change the world?

— Steve Jobs

A Rainmaker Is Born

He who masters storytelling rules the world.

— Wipala Wiki

I was a very scared little boy. It was the Fourth of July, 1955, and we were camped on the banks of Bray Creek under the Mogollon Rim — my father, his brother George, their 'Blood Brother' Wipala Wiki, and me. We had been hiking all day, fishing, exploring, and hunting for arrowheads.

Now we were seated, Indian style, around a blazing campfire. The night was black, the moon was full, and there were mountain lions and bears out there somewhere, but it was not the mountain lions and bears that scared me. Lethal lightning could come from the thundering skies when the Great Spirit was angry! I had heard about people being struck and killed by lightning, and *that's* what scared me.

Thunder and lightning had always scared me, but that night I was more frightened than usual — maybe because, earlier in the day, Wipala had mentioned that night we would have a "white man's moon" and I wondered what that meant and if it had anything to do with me.

Wipala Wiki sat staring into the fire as he shared his stories. His strong face was etched by almost eighty years of Arizona sun, and his heart and mind were filled with stories that were legendary. Occasionally, he would look up at one of us with his piercing eyes to monitor our reactions.
He always started by telling the story of his life and would begin by looking at me and smiling.

At birth, he had become the hereditary chief of the Antelope Clan of the Hopi people. Most of his stories were about an apocalypse that had started with the arrival of the white man. Wipala told us that we were at the very end of our trail. He told us to look up at the moon, and that someday a white man would go to the moon and bring something back. I was mesmerized by Wipala.

That night, Wipala told us about the two paths depicted on the famous Hopi Prophecy Rock: the 'two-hearted' path and the 'one-hearted' path. Per Hopi legend, a 'two-hearted' person is one who thinks with his head rather than his heart, leading to imbalance and inner conflict; a 'one-hearted' person thinks with his heart and is in balance and harmony with the universe.

The Hopi Prophecy Rock shows a junction where the two-hearted people have a clear choice to start thinking with their hearts or continue thinking with their heads. Continuing to think with their heads will lead them to self-destruction, symbolized by a lightning bolt from a cloud.

The Hopis believed that greed, a 'terrible sickness,' would cause people to lose respect for the Great Spirit and Mother Earth and that would end the world. These days many people are without any spiritual grounding, and many have lost respect for our environment. Perhaps some of the Hopi prophecies have already come true.

The Hopis had a lot of prophecies, none of which seemed to make all that much sense to an eight-year-old. I wished I was back home safe in my warm bed, but was hypnotized by Wipala as he transported me through time and space, fantasy and reality. He started talking about the rituals, ceremonies, and songs of the Snake people and ancient rainmakers, and then — exactly then — lightning lit up the sky and thunder roared and echoed across the Mogollon Rim. I wondered if the Great Spirit was angry with me. It was a strange feeling.

Wipala Wiki's stories made a lasting impact on my life. All his stories had in common the message that we all must take responsibility for whatever is in our sphere of influence. Like Wipala, I choose to take the 'one-hearted' path — in thinking with my heart and being in balance and harmony with the universe. God created us with the power of awareness and with it the wisdom and passion of continuing to seek a newer world.

I agree that we have may have arrived at the end of our trail, but that doesn't mean that we are at the end of our lives or the end of our civilization. It means that we are about to experience a great renaissance — a new age of innovation, social entrepreneurship, social and environmental responsibility, and Rainmaking. There has never been a better time for all of us to become Rainmakers and positively impact the world.

Ancient Hopi rainmakers brought more than rain; they brought hope. As Rainmakers, we must respect the Great Spirit, whatever we believe it to be, and respect Mother Earth. We can leverage the power of emotions and the magic of storytelling to impact the world. Let's think with our hearts, remembering the Hopi proverb: "The rain falls on the just and the unjust."

I survived that night of lightning and thunder and returned to the safety of my native Southern California beaches. I visited the Mogollon Rim many more times, but I always remembered the Night of the White Man's Moon — it was the night that I began my path from a boy to a man. Before that, my world revolved around surfing and the other things we did growing up in the Fifties, like playing baseball, reading science fiction, and watching movies about how we won World War II. Wipala had started me thinking about my life.

That summer changed my life in other ways: when we returned from Arizona, my family visited Disneyland on opening day. We walked down Main Street for the first time and experienced the four lands of Walt Disney's Magical Kingdom: Fantasyland, Frontierland, Adventureland, and Tomorrowland. It was that day that my world expanded far beyond the beaches of California and the mountains of Arizona. I was in a world where characters are bigger-than-life and dreams become reality.

I would continue through my "Wonder Years" and "Happy Days." Despite tragedies and personal disappointments, I never stopped dreaming. One of my heroes, President Kennedy, would be killed, and I would lose friends in Vietnam. I would fall in and out of love more than once; the faces, words, thoughts, and dreams of my life would come and go. But, in that summer of 1955, two great Rainmakers, Wipala Wiki and Walt Disney, forever influenced my life and my future path.

Rainmaking 101

Demasiada cordura puede ser locura
y la mayor locura de todas es ver la vida
como es y no como debería ser.

(Too much sanity may be madness
and the maddest of all,
to see life as it is and not as it should be.)

— Miguel de Cervantes

A horse walks into a bar, and a salesman starts selling him insurance. The horse turns to leave and a Rainmaker, hearing the encounter, stops the horse and asks him: "Why the long face?"

The difference between a salesman and a Rainmaker is that salesmen 'pitch' everyone they meet; Rainmakers are trained to start out by discovering *why* people feel the way they do. Salesmen start selling without knowing or caring much about the other person. Rainmakers establish trust through learning about people and empathizing, and then begin influencing people.

I wrote this book to inspire you to use your passion, energy, and talent to make a positive impact on others. *Rainmaking* is not about making money; it's about making an impact: make an impact, and the money will come — contribute to making a newer world, and you'll be rewarded beyond your wildest imaginings.

When I was a boy, Dick Tracy and his pals wore two-way wrist radios, and The Jetsons rode in electric cars. Telephones had dials, and we used slide rules to calculate. Now, gadgets are sexier and more elegant. They affect how we think, feel, and act. We're empowered well beyond the imagination of Jules Verne. Innovators have taken us 'through the looking glass' into a new and exciting world where we're all connected. Now, we can instantaneously penetrate ideologies and cross political and cultural borders. We are free in a lot of ways but also enslaved by technology.

We have the personal and social power to make a new world — one where everybody is free and safe and secure, and nobody is hungry or homeless or without medical attention, energy, transportation, or education. We have learned that we can't depend on politicians to do it for us, and we don't want them to. Each of us must embrace the challenge and assume personal responsibility to innovate and influence.

What do we do with our time and talent? That's a question that each of us should ask ourselves — if it's just all about making money for you, most of the strategies in this book will help you earn money. I hope, however, that you will do more than that — I hope you will make an impact.

Everyone is selling something: either you are selling a product or service, an idea or ideology, or you are selling yourself. Forget everything you think you know about selling. Between the past and the future, between dreams and reality, you are about to enter the dimension of innovation and influence called *Rainmaking*.

By believing in Rainmaking, your life will change, and you will impact the world by influencing the lives of others. If God didn't put you on earth to make an impact, why are you here?

Combined with your personal passion, charisma, and energy, *Rainmaking* has the power to impact your life in an amazing way. I am going to give you everything you need to become a great Rainmaker; the rest is up to you.

Rainmaking is 'raw and unplugged,' with no apologies. I realize that this book is different than what you may be used to reading. There are a lot of things in here that may not make sense to you; many of them don't make a lot of sense to me — I just know they *work*.

I have neither tried to offend anyone in this book nor toned down anything to be politically correct. My personal style has always been to use a lot of stories, analogies, and jokes. I try not to use clichés, except in cases where a cliché is the best way to get a point across. Keep in mind that words can be intense, and it's not the words, but how the words are used.

The quotes, song lyrics, and stories in *Rainmaking* are here for their impact value. All of them have made some memorable impact on me. If you read something that evokes feelings from you, that's good; stop right there and ask yourself *why* you're feeling what you're feeling.

Rainmakers are word masters; we know how to use words for their maximum impact. That is the key to Rainmaking.

I believe in Never-never Land. Like the hippies and flower children of the Sixties and most Miss Universe candidates, I believe in world peace and an end to world hunger. I also believe in a world where the New York Yankees win the World Series every year, and everyone is a vegan, but I know that you'll eventually wake up from Never-never Land, leave Disneyland, crawl out of from behind the looking glass, or return to Kansas.

Then, you're in a *real* world where almost everyone wants to get something from you, punch you until you are down, and, keep kicking you if they can. As negative as that might sound, it's often true. Not everyone is 'paying it forward' for you when you are in line at Starbucks.

Rainmaking will show you how to break free from the ordinary world and change yourself from an order-taker or everyday salesperson into a powerful and impactful Rainmaker in a world full of opportunity of your own making.

This book is all about *you* and *your* power to become a Rainmaker — to impact the world through the power of emotions and the magic of storytelling. Reading *Rainmaking* is merely the first step in an ongoing process of personal and professional growth. Becoming a great Rainmaker will require more than *reading* this book. To succeed, you will need to understand the process of Rainmaking and believe in the power of emotion and magic of storytelling. And you will need to act.

Through the years, I have noticed many people get excited about something and then become disinterested or discouraged when the ether wears off. If you have ever been to a motivational meeting or seminar, you know what I mean. People jump up and down in their seats, holler at the top of their lungs, exchange high-fives and fist-bumps, walk on hot coals, and break into tears. When that magic of the moment vaporizes, reality begins to set in.

What do you do when the music stops playing? What do you do when you hit the wall? What do you do when you feel all alone? Where do you get the strength when you feel like you don't care about anything anymore? That's the one thing I can't tell you. That's the one thing you must discover yourself.

Maybe you'll find that strength and inspiration in God. Maybe you'll find that strength somewhere else. Whatever you must do, don't ever let the magic vaporize. *You* are the magic. God gave you everything you need to be a great Rainmaker — NOW you are going to make it happen. Take the 'one hearted path' and follow your heart and you'll never lose the magic.

Now let's learn about the power of emotions.

Part I: Emotions

Remember: The key to persuasion is softening people up and breaking them down, gently. Seduce them with a two-pronged approach. Work on their emotions and play on their intellectual weaknesses. Be alert to both what separates them from everybody else (their individual psychology) and what they share with everyone else (their basic emotional responses). Aim at the primary emotions, love, hate, jealousy. Once you move their emotions you have reduced their control, making them more vulnerable to persuasion.

— Robert Greene
The 48 Laws of Power

We are trained to think that people act or fail to act for logical reasons. Logic only provides us with confusing (and often conflicting) information. In the end, we are all creatures of emotion. We must retrain ourselves to empathize and to follow our *hearts*, not our minds.

Emotions make the world go 'round. There are positive emotions and negative emotions, and some emotions (like passion) can play either role. Rainmaking works by touching people's emotions through storytelling and making them open to being persuaded to act.

People are guided by their emotions when making decisions. They intake information and process it, but their actions (or lack thereof) are based on what they *feel*. Great Rainmakers understand the role that emotions play in influencing people. Mastering emotions is one of the underlying principles of modern Rainmaking.

Emotions can be powerful drivers or enormous roadblocks. The key to leveraging other people's emotions is being in control of your own. It is equally important to empathize with their raw feelings without being patronizing.

All our emotions — our feelings — begin in our brain. Our brain, weighing only about three pounds, is our most powerful organ. It is made up of several parts that work together to process the information we receive. The part of the brain that regulates our emotions is the limbic system.

Our *limbic system* controls our emotions, memories, and stimulation. Our emotions are controlled by the levels of certain chemicals in our brain. Our brain, having the texture of firm jelly, is a complex network which controls information and sends signals via neurotransmitters. Our brain processes the present, memories of past experiences, and preconceived ideas and expectations.

The *amygdala* is an integrative center controlling our motivation, emotions, and emotional behavior. It is the starting point for fear and anxiety, which occur when environmental factors or stressors signal that we are in danger. Here is how the chain reaction works: the stressors signal the amygdala to prepare for 'fight or flight,' and epinephrine is released into our bloodstream. We all know what happens next: the amygdala wants to keep us safe (and usually does).

Dopamine is a chemical that is released by nerve cells in our brain and transmitted to other nerve cells in our body. It's a neurotransmitter which plays a major role in reward-motivated behavior. *Dopamine* gives us a feeling of accomplishment when we close a deal or finish a race — it is known as 'the pleasure chemical' that gives us that natural high that we all love and desire.

Serotonin, also a neurotransmitter, is known as 'the calming chemical' and makes us feel focused and relaxed. It is a major contributor to making us feel happy.

Oxytocin, a hormone, is an endorphin which functions as a natural pain reliever which masks pain and helps reduce stress in our body. It gives us a sense of safety and is especially important at the beginning of our relationships.

Cortisol, a steroid hormone, is produced in the adrenal cortex of our brain. It is produced in response to stress or anxiety and functions to increase our blood sugar in the first stage of 'flight or fight.'

Our emotions are linked to and necessary for all the decisions we make. Without our emotions and feelings, we would be unable to distinguish between rational and irrational behavior. Time also plays an important role: the more quickly we decide, the more confident we feel; the longer it takes, the less confident we feel. Every decision involves emotions at some level.

People act when their emotions tell them to act. That does not mean that using negative emotions to control people is right, but it *does* mean that you need understand *why* people make decisions: our emotions drive our actions. And, you must learn to master your own emotions.

Positive Emotions

Love

**And in the end, the love you take
Is equal to the love you make**

— The End — The Beatles
John Lennon and Paul McCartney (1969)

Safety

**Your own safety is at risk when your neighbor's wall
is ablaze.**

— Horace

We all want to feel safe. Safety and security are
the flip side of danger and fear. The need for
security plays an enormous role in the decisions
we make, every minute of every day. If we feel
safe, we want to stay safe; if we are threatened,
we want to quickly get to a safe place.

We can usually determine how safe and secure
other people feel by their nonverbal indicators.
Their body language reveals if they are afraid or
uncomfortable. A Rainmaker can see fear in
people's eyes; their eyes can tell you if they feel
relaxed and safe with you. And their words and
voice patterns are indications of their emotions.

21

Desire

A child's appetite for new toys appeals to the desire for ownership and appropriation: the appeal of toys comes to lie not in their use but in their status as possessions.

— Christopher Lash

Desire drives action forward. If they already want what you have, you are 90% there. People wish for things for many different reasons. Your job isn't to uncover what they want; they'll tell you if you just ask them. As a Rainmaker, your job is to determine *why* they want it and how they feel about getting it (or not).

Excitement

Money was never a big motivation for me, except as a way to keep score. The real excitement is playing the game.

— Donald Trump

Excitement is contagious. Excitement is the catalyst that opens and closes deals. Set the deal up right; add your excitement; get them excited, and *voilà* — you are Rainmaking!

Satisfaction

When I'm watchin' my TV
And that man comes on to tell me
How white my shirts can be
But he can't be a man 'cause he doesn't smoke
The same cigarettes as me
I can't get no, oh no no no
Hey hey hey, that's what I say
I can't get no satisfaction.

> — *(I Can't Get No) Satisfaction* — The Rolling Stones
> Mick Jagger and Keith Richards (1965)

Rainmakers don't want people to have any concerns after a commitment is made — they must remain satisfied.

Belief

I have never worked a day in my life without selling. If I believe in something, I sell it, and I sell it hard.

> — Estée Lauder

All caterpillars start out believing that someday they will fly; the ones that stop believing die. Rainmakers *believe.*

Gratitude

Gratitude is giving more than you can and pride is taking less than you need.

— Khalil Gibran

Gratitude is amazing: to be a Rainmaker, give more than you think you can, take less than you think you need, and be grateful. Always.

Happiness

Advertising is based on one thing, happiness. And you know what happiness is? Happiness is the smell of a new car. It's freedom from fear. It's a billboard on the side of the road that screams reassurance that whatever you are doing is okay. You are okay.

— Don Draper (Jon Hamm)
Mad Men (Season 1)

Happiness sells. Happy people sign on the dotted line without looking back. Rainmakers find out what makes people happy and give it to them. It's that simple!

Pride

I'm a black American, I am proud of my race. I am proud of who I am. I have a lot of pride and dignity.

— Michael Jackson

Pride can be good or bad. As a Rainmaker, you can play into other people's pride. Recognize them. Applaud them. Make them feel special.

People can be proud of many different things. People can be proud of their achievements or the accomplishments of others. By discovering the sources of people's pride, you can tap into their feelings. Pride is a powerful positive emotion but beware of false pride which can be misleading and have adverse effects.

Accomplishment

You're born, you take shit. You get out in the world, you take more shit. You climb a little higher, you take less shit. Till one day you're up in the rarefied atmosphere and you've forgotten what shit even looks like. Welcome to the layer cake son.

— Eddie Temple (Michael Gambon)
A Layer Cake (2004)

Accomplishment is a wonderful feeling. There's no feeling like reaching the top of the mountain.

Courage

Let me tell you something you already know. The world ain't all sunshine and rainbows. It is a very mean and nasty place and it will beat you to your knees and keep you there permanently if you let it. You, me, or nobody is gonna hit as hard as life. But it ain't how hard you hit; it's about how hard you can get hit, and keep moving forward. How much you can take, and keep moving forward. That's how winning is done. Now, if you know what you're worth, then go out and get what you're worth. But you gotta be willing to take the hit, and not pointing fingers saying you ain't where you are because of him, or her, or anybody. Cowards do that and that ain't you. You're better than that.

— Rocky Balboa (Sylvester Stallone)
Rocky Balboa (2006)

Trust

I can get a good look at a T-bone by sticking my head up a bull's ass, but I'd rather take the butcher's word for it.

— Tommy (Chris Farley)
Tommy Boy (1995)

Trust is a Rainmaker's greatest asset in getting people to take the actions you want them to take. It begins the first second that someone hears about you, reads about you, or meets you.

Passion

Do it no matter what. If you believe in it, it is
something very honorable. If somebody around you
or your family does not understand it, then that's
their problem. But if you do have a passion, an
honest passion, just do it.

— Mario Andretti

Passion can't be faked. Passion is my favorite
word and my favorite emotion. Passion is a
wonderful emotion and a very hard feeling to
describe. Passion can excite you, enthrall you,
drive you, and anger you. Passion can act as a
catalyst when added to any other emotion. Like
pride, passion can be a double-edged sword.
Passion can drive Rainmakers to greatness or
passion can destroy them. Be passionate, but be
aware of both the power and danger of passion.

Negative Emotions

Confusion

Sixty minutes of thinking of any kind is bound to lead to confusion and unhappiness.

— James Thurber

Confusion can be mental and emotional. People's thoughts can be confused, and feelings can be conflicting. Confusion paralyzes. Confusion is a multidimensional emotion that can range from mild to extreme. Rainmakers attack people's confusion and help them feel good about making decisions and acting.

Doubt

Alice: **This is impossible.**
The Mad Hatter: **Only if you believe it is.**

— Lewis Carroll
Alice in Wonderland

Doubt is a haunting feeling — every Rainmaker's nightmare. As J. M. Barrie's *Peter Pan* said: "The moment you doubt whether you can fly, you cease forever to be able to do it."

Pain

Any thought that causes you pain, is the cause of the pain.
Believing the thought — increases pain.
Questioning the thought — releases pain.

— Donnie Wahlberg

Pain hurts. Physical pain is an indicator that something is horribly wrong with our body. Mental pain torments us emotionally and causes us to suffer,

Question thoughts that cause pain. Rainmakers know that, as Charlie Chan (Sidney Toler) said in *Charlie Chan at Treasure Island,* "Great happiness follows great pain."

Hate

Let no man pull you so low as to hate him.

— Martin Luther King, Jr.

Hate is the ugliest emotion; for that reason, I don't even like writing about it. As a Rainmaker, I am not sure that I have ever hated, although I have *been* hated. Do not get involved with hate. Hate has no place in Rainmaking.

Anger

**Every day we have plenty of opportunities to get
angry, stressed or offended. But what you're doing
when you indulge these negative emotions is giving
something outside yourself power over your
happiness. You can choose to not let little things
upset you.**

— Joel Osteen

Anger can be a great motivator, driving people to
act and make decisions. Anger can also cause
people to be stubborn and do nothing.

Rainmakers must be able to understand *why*
people are angry. Also make sure that you always
control your own anger — uncontrolled anger can
cause you to think, feel, and act irrationally.

Shame

Shame has poor memory.

— Gabriel García Márquez
In Evil Hour

Shame is often short-lived, but it can hide deep in
our souls for a lifetime. To determine how you can
leverage this soul-eating emotion, you must
discover *why* people are ashamed and the level
and intensity of their shame.

Regret

We're so sorry, Uncle Albert.
We're so sorry if we caused you any pain.

— *Uncle Albert/Admiral Halsey* — The Beatles
Paul and Linda McCartney (1971)

One of the main reasons people delay decisions or refuse to make deals is that they don't want to regret their decisions. Rainmakers turn the situation around by showing them that they will regret *not* doing the deal. People want to feel good about what they do.

Uncertainty

When player cannot see man who deals cards, much wiser to stay out of game.

— Charlie Chan (Warner Orland)
Charlie Chan at the Race Track (1936)

Uncertainty makes people worry. Many people stay out of a deal when they are uncertain. Being uncertain often makes people think the worst, and that is especially true when money is involved.

Your challenge is to do everything you can to ensure that people are not uncertain about your integrity, and your motives. Making people *believe* in you helps alleviate some of their uncertainty.

31

Envy

Envy blinds men and makes it impossible for them to think clearly.

— Malcolm X

Envy makes people crazy. Envious people do crazy things, and envious people often make poor decisions. Envious people can also make excellent decisions. It's important for Rainmakers to determine the details of the envy: the who, what, when, and why.

You are on a fishing boat in the Gulf of Mexico, one of a dozen boats bobbing in the ocean as the sun rises in the east. The boats are close enough to see the other people and you notice that they're hauling in big fish like crazy. What are you thinking? How are you feeling? Are you envious of them? Do you wish you were on one of the other boats? The good news is that the fish are biting!

Insecurity

I have self-doubt. I have insecurity. I have fear of failure. I have nights when I show up at the arena and I'm like, 'My back hurts, my feet hurt, my knees hurt. I don't have it. I just want to chill.' We all have self-doubt. You don't deny it, but you also don't capitulate to it. You embrace it.

— Kobe Bryant

If Kobe Bryant feels insecure sometimes, expect almost everyone (including yourself) to feel insecure at one time or another. Follow Kobe's advice: "You embrace it." All you must do is to make people feel secure and you'll have a deal!

Greed

The point is that you can't be too greedy.

— Donald Trump

"Danger, Will Robinson!" *(Lost in Space)* — greed can be extremely dangerous.

"Danger, Rainmaker!" Greed is a super-strong emotion that can shoot your deal to the moon or drive it into the ground. There is nothing wrong with leveraging off other people's greed; just be careful not to allow greed to consume you.

Anxiety

I hear ev'ry mother say
Mother needs something today to calm her down
And though she's not really ill
There's a little yellow pill

> — *Mother's Little Helper* — The Rolling Stones
> Mick Jagger and Keith Richards (1966)

Anxiety is a killer, but it can also be a great deal maker. Rainmakers find out why others are anxious and how they feel about it. Are they are suffering from chronic anxiety, or is their anxiety directly related to your deal? If it is, you're almost home free. If it's related to something else, you will have some work to do.

Fear

Aubrey, I've known the fear of losing, but now I am almost too frightened to win.

> — Harold M. Abrahams (Ben Cross)
> *Chariots of Fire* (1981)

Fear is an emotional monster. If you want to be a Rainmaker, you must not be afraid. The monster must not win!

The Tells

Tells are what people consciously and unconsciously communicate verbally and non-verbally. Tells are indicators of people's emotions, which encompasses their feelings, thoughts, attitudes, and moods. Tells can help you read people at any given moment, including their characteristics and personality traits. Send an email to: Robert@RobertMillerNOW.com for a free PDF, *A Rainmaker's Guide to the Tells*.

Words and Phrases

- truthfully, to be truthful with you
- frankly, to be frank with you
- honestly, to be honest with you
- actually
- any profanity

Body Language

- eyes — the #1 Tell
- facial expressions and micro expressions
- posture and movements
- the position of the body
- breathing, heartbeat, perspiration, blushing
- the odors emitted by the body
- how and what people touch
- eating and drinking habits and choices
- perceived health and wellness
- hand movements, gestures, positioning

Appearance

- their manner of dress
- personal grooming (nails)
- style and condition of shoes
- jewelry (bling, religious or spiritual artifacts)
- tattoos, piercings, hair styling and coloring

The Voice

- volume, pitch, and tone
- pace, pauses, and variation
- sound frequencies creating vibrations
- control and modulation
- speed — nervously rushed or slowed

Nervous Habits

- finger tapping and foot tapping
- nail biting and lip biting
- nervous smoking or drinking
- grinding and clenching teeth
- sucking or chewing pens or pencils
- playing with hair (or facial hair)
- cracking knuckles
- touching the face
- uncontrolled laughing or giggling
- coughing
- twitching
- laughing
- stuttering
- darting eyes

Emotional Energy

- the intensity of people's presence
- the strength of a handshake or hug
- gut feelings
- crying
- laughing
- excitement
- intuitive empathy

There are many different opinions on the role that words, body language, and voice play in the process of communicating. I believe that all three-combined account for only one-half of all communication. Here are my estimates: words (5%), body language (25%), and voice (20%). **Emotional energy accounts for 50% of people's communication.**

Because the face is the most accurate indicator of a person's emotions, Rainmakers must especially master the interpretation of facial expressions (micro expressions). The best way to do that is to look at yourself in the mirror and mimic some facial expressions. When you put an expression on your face, you will begin to feel the emotion. Emotions cause expressions and expressions can cause emotions.

Before you can even think about becoming a great Rainmaker, you must master your emotions. You must be in control of your personal Tells.

Part II: Storytelling

Today everyone, whether they know it or not, is in the emotional transportation business. More and more, success is won by creating compelling stories that have the power to move people to action. Simply put, if you can't tell it, you can't sell it.

— Peter Guber

ONCE UPON A TIME are the four words that begin a lot of stories, but they all have different endings. Great stories not only tell you who, what and when. They tell you *why*.

Storytelling is an art, not a science. Everyone has their stories, and everyone has their ways of telling them. Some stories are amazing — inspiring delight, pleasure, desire, or admiration. Other stories are terrible — provoking effects that are extremely unpleasant or disagreeable.

Stories can magically transport you and your emotions to anywhere the storyteller wants to take you. Stories can be straightforward and entertaining, or they can have very profound messages either above or below the surface. Stories can provoke thoughts and actions.

Your effectiveness as a Rainmaker depends on your story-making skills. You must be creative, captivating, and credible (with the accent on *credible*). If people don't believe you, you'll be wasting your time.

In the words of Taylor Swift:

"You can draw inspiration from anything. If you're a good storyteller, you can take a dirty look somebody gives you, or if a guy you used to have flirtations with starts dating a new girl, or somebody you're casually talking to says something that makes you so mad — you can create an entire scenario around that."

Make your stories brief and entertaining. Be in tune with your audience and aware of how you can impact their thoughts, beliefs, and emotions. If you choose to exaggerate or improvise, be sure you know what you're doing — there is a fine line between 'just enough' and 'too much.'

The following stories all contain important messages for Rainmakers to incorporate into deal-making. After you read each one, take a minute to consider how a Rainmaker might use it to the best advantage.

The opening narration for *Beauty and the Beast* is a perfect example of a Rainmaking story. This story grabs your attention by immediately getting you emotionally involved. You are emotionally transported into the castle and empathize with the beast: "For who could ever love a beast?"

In *the Carousel Don Draper* (*Mad Men*) presented an ad campaign for the Kodak Slide Projector and emotionally transported us "to a place we ache to go again." In *the Hershey Bar*. Draper addressed a group of executives from The Hershey Company and shared a personal story that leaves us wondering if it happened.

Let's look at the stories.

Beauty and the Beast

Once upon a time, in a faraway land, a young prince lived in a shining castle. Although he had everything his heart desired, the prince was spoiled, selfish, and unkind. But then, one winter's night, an old beggar woman came to the castle and offered him a single rose in return for shelter from the bitter cold. Repulsed by her haggard appearance, the prince sneered at the gift and turned the old woman away. She warned him not to be deceived by appearance, for beauty is found within. When he dismissed her a second time, the old woman's ugliness melted away to reveal a beautiful enchantress. The prince tried to apologize but it was too late, for she had seen that there was no love in his heart. As punishment, she transformed him into a hideous beast and placed a powerful spell on the castle and all who lived there. Ashamed of his monstrous form, the beast concealed himself inside his castle, with a magic mirror as his only window to the outside world. The rose she offered was truly an enchanted rose, which would bloom until his twenty-first year. If he could earn her love in return by the time the last petal fell, then the spell would be broken. If not, he would be doomed to remain a beast for all time. As the years passed, he fell into despair and lost all hope. For who could ever love a beast?

— [*opening narration*] *Beauty and the Beast* (1991)

The Orgastic Future

I remembered how we'd all come to Gatsby's and guessed at his corruption while he stood before us concealing an incorruptible dream. The moon rose higher and, as I stood there brooding on the old unknown world, I thought of Gatsby's wonder when he first picked out the green light at the end of Daisy's dock. He had come such a long way, and his dream must have seemed so close that he could hardly fail to grasp it. But he did not know that it was already behind him. Gatsby believed in the green light, the orgastic future that year by year recedes before us. It eluded us then — but that's no matter — tomorrow we will run faster, stretch out our arms farther . . . And one fine morning — So we beat on, boats against the current, borne back ceaselessly into the past.

— Nick Carraway (Tobey Maguire)
The Great Gatsby [*final scene*] (2013)

The Carousel

Well, technology is a glittering lure. But there is a rare occasion when the public can be engaged on a level beyond flash — if they have a sentimental bond with the product. My first job was in-house at a fur company, with this old pro of a copywriter, a Greek, named Teddy. Teddy told me the most important idea in advertising is 'new.' It creates an itch. You simply put your product in there as a kind of calamine lotion. He also talked about a deeper bond with a product: nostalgia. It's delicate but potent. Sweetheart. [*Draper addresses his assistant, and she starts a slideshow featuring photos of his family*]. Teddy told me that, in Greek, nostalgia literally means the pain from an old wound. It's a twinge in your heart, far more powerful than memory alone. This device isn't a space ship, it's a time machine. It goes backwards, forwards. It takes us to a place where we ache to go again. It's not called the wheel; it's called the carousel. It lets us travel the way a child travels. Round and round, and back home again. To a place where we know we are loved.

— Don Draper (Jon Hamm)
Mad Men (Season 1)

The Hershey Bar

[*addressing a group of executives from The Hershey Company*]

Don: I was an orphan. I grew up in Pennsylvania, in a whorehouse. I read about Milton Hershey and his school in Coronet magazine or some other crap the girls left by the toilet. And I read that some orphans had a different life there. I could picture it. I dreamt of it — of being wanted. Because the woman who was forced to raise me would look at me every day like she hoped I would disappear. Closest I got to feeling wanted was from a girl who made me go through her john's pockets while they screwed. If I collected more than a dollar, she'd buy me a Hershey bar. And I would eat it alone in my room with great ceremony [*choking up*] . . . feeling like a normal kid. It said 'sweet' on the package. It was the only sweet thing in my life.

Hershey's executive: [*aghast*] You want to advertise that?

Don: If I had it my way you would never advertise. You shouldn't have someone like me telling that boy what a Hershey's bar is. He already knows.

— Don Draper (Jon Hamm)
Mad Men (Season 6)

45

ROBERT MILLER

Las Vegas

There was this kid I grew up with; he was younger
than me. Sorta looked up to me, you know? We
did our first work together; we worked our way
out of the street. Things were good — we made
the most of it. During Prohibition, we ran
molasses into Canada . . . made a fortune — your
father, too. As much as anyone, I loved him and
trusted him. Later, he had an idea to build a city
out of a desert stopover for GIs on the way to the
West Coast. That kid's name was Moe Greene,
and the city he invented was Las Vegas. This was
a great man, a man of vision and guts. And there
isn't even a plaque or a signpost or a statue of
him in that town! Someone put a bullet through
his eye. When I heard it, I wasn't angry; I knew
Moe. I knew he was headstrong; talking loud;
saying stupid things. So, when he turned up dead,
I let it go. And, I said to myself, this is the
business we've chosen; I didn't ask who gave the
order, because it had nothing to do with business.

— Hyman Roth (Lee Strasberg)
The Godfather: Part II (1974)

46

Hollywood

How did a postcard that I received as a free bonus from a headshot company turn into a hundred Gs? Years ago, I read a book about making a living as a working actor in L.A. It wasn't about becoming a star, but about making a good living as an actor (which is doable). I decided to implement what I learned from the book. The author merely suggested sending a polite postcard to all the local casting directors that I would like to work with and wait for their response. I sent out the cards and waited for two years for a response from a casting director that is known for great jobs. I was so happy when I finally got a call from this casting director for an acting job! But alas… just as an extra. I took the job, as it paid well and got me on the roster of the casting agency. I showed up at the set with a positive attitude and noticed that I was being treated exceptionally well for an extra. It just so happened that the director 'upgraded' me from an extra to a principal actor. The commercial went on to become a worldwide smash, and I made over $100,000 in residuals from that one job. Never underestimate the power of a free postcard.

— Jay Diamond

47

ROBERT MILLER

Meeting Harry

One bitterly cold January day in 1979, when I was
a budding singer/songwriter exploring the folk
music scene in Greenwich Village, I was walking
down West 3rd Street in a too-thin jacket with my
hands in my pockets and my head bowed to
escape a biting wind when I ran smack into a
mountain of a human being. When I looked up to
apologize, I realized that I had collided with one of
my personal heroes — none other than folk
superstar Harry Chapin! Being both winded and
star struck, I burbled something unintelligible and
immediately felt myself flush with embarrassment.

After asking if I was alright (I was so tongue-tied
that I could only nod 'yes'), Chapin put his hand
on my shoulder and said "Tell me about yourself,
young man." I replied "Oh, Mr. Chapin …), to
which he interjected "Call me Harry." Beginning
again, I blurted out: "Oh, Harry . . . if I had one-
tenth of the talent in my whole body that you have
in your little finger, I would be in the music
industry, just like you!"

What I felt next was absolutely unlike anything I
have felt before or since. Through the enormous
hand on my shoulder, I felt a seismic rumble that I
quickly realized was the beginning of a huge belly
laugh. It seemed to take a full minute or more to
ripen, and then it burst forth with astonishing, full-

48

throated vigor. After wiping tears away from the corners of his sparkling eyes, Harry, at long last, spoke: "Son — suh . . . huh . . . HUNN — you don't need talent to be in the music industry — you just need to be able to tell a story well!" With that, he released my shoulder and ambled off down the street, chuckling to himself.

I have been performing all over the world for more than forty years now, and in all of that time, Harry's one line of advice remains the best that anyone has ever given me about how to reach an audience. I have looked for the story in every song I have sung since that day, and doing so has connected me with thousands of people from all walks of life and in cultures completely foreign to my own.

Harry Chapin was a masterful storyteller in song, and I have always been grateful that he took a moment on a frigid New York City morning all those years ago to show me his titan heart and to pass along the lasting gift of appreciation for the power of a well-told story, perfectly set in time and place.

— Rich Follett

Part III: Strategies

You outwork, outthink, out scheme and outmaneuver. You make no friends. You trust nobody. And you make damn sure you're the smartest guy in the room whenever the subject of money comes up.

— Uncle Pat (Ron Dean)
Cocktail (1988)

1 | Discover Your Why

All these non-singing, non-dancing, wish-I-had some-clothes fools who tell me my albums suck. Why should I pay attention to them?

— Prince

It's not enough to believe in yourself. Rainmakers must know *why* they believe in themselves.

It's important to give credit where credit is due. From my first draft of this book until just now, Strategy #1 was "Fuggedaboutit" As I was editing this book, I thought about Simon Sinek. I have watched most of his videos many times. Simon is a captivating and fascinating presenter. What impresses me is his concept of "start with the why". And so, I have bumped "Fuggedaboutit!" to Strategy #2. Thanks, Simon.

Check out SIMON SINEK at TED.com.

Today, as I was revising this page, Prince was found dead in an elevator at his Paisley Park complex. If you listen to the lyrics of *Let's Go Crazy*, you will hear Prince sing: "and if the elevator tries to bring you down. Go crazy — punch a higher floor." RIP Prince.

2 | Fuggedaboutit!

"Forget about it" is, like, if you agree with someone, you know, like "Raquel Welch is one great piece of ass. Forget about it!" But then, if you disagree, like "A Lincoln is better than a Cadillac? Forget about it!" You know? But then, it's also like if something's the greatest thing in the world, like, "Minghia! Those peppers! Forget about it!" But it's also like saying "Go to hell!" too. Like, you know, like "Hey Paulie, you got a one-inch pecker? And Paulie says "Forget about it!" Sometimes it just means "Forget about it."

— Donnie Brasco (Johnny Depp)
Donnie Brasco (1997)

Forget everything!

I know that it's easier said than done. Short of drug-induced amnesia, we are unable to lose or inhibit the creation of unwanted memories, but we can take all that bad stuff and create a new file in our brain and move it there, if only temporarily.

Clear your mind of everything you think you know about selling, deal-making, rainmaking, or even life. It no longer matters what you have learned in the past about handling objections and alternative closes.

3 | Know What a Rainmaker Is

Rainmakers are born, not made. Rainmakers are innovators who impact the world through the power of emotions and the magic of storytelling.

Modern Rainmakers:

Tony Robbins — Life Changer
Joel Osteen — Motivator
Oprah Winfrey — Influencer
Simon Sinek — Creative Thinker
Walt Disney — Imagineer
Paul Simon — Storyteller
J.K. Rowling — Dreamweaver

What they do not know is that the rain seeks me. It is my tempest that they see.

— Deck Shiffler (Danny DeVito)
The Rainmaker

You know what a Rainmaker is, kid? The bucks are gonna be falling from the sky.

— John William Corrington
The Rainmaker (1997)

Who is the greatest Rainmaker that you know personally? What qualities do you most admire about him/her?

4 | Know What a Rainmaker Isn't

A bad salesman will automatically drop his price.
Bad salesmen make me sick.

> — Sam Stone (Danny DeVito)
> *Ruthless People* (1966)

Rainmakers can't be self-proclaimed.

Pop Culture Characters who aren't Rainmakers:

Bernie Madoff — *Madoff*
Blake — *Glengarry Glen Ross*
Gordon Gekko — *Wall Street; Wall Street: Money Never Sleeps*
John Gray — *9 ½ Weeks*
Jordan Belfort — *The Wolf of Wall Street*
Patrick Bateman — *American Psycho*

Do you know anyone who displays a pervasive pattern of disregard for the safety and rights of others? How do you feel after interacting with this person?

5 | Define Who You Are

By God, I shall be a king. This is the time of King Arthur. When we shall — reach for the stars! This is the time of King Arthur when violence is not strength and compassion is not weakness.

— King Arthur (Richard Harris)
Camelot (1967)

You are who you choose to be. Be real about defining who you are and about how other people define themselves.

I'm a rainmaker. I make it rain...

— Bernie Madoff (Richard Dreyfuss)
Madoff (2016)

Watch the YouTube video showing Richard Harris in *Camelot* (1967) delivering the lines: "By God, I shall be a king." How is he defining himself with this famous line?

Defining who you are involves your beliefs, values, and ethics. It may, or may not, have something to do with what you do. It has more to do with why you do it. King Arthur was a great Rainmaker. Bernie Madoff is not.

6 | Decide What You're Selling

The only thing you've got in this world is what you can sell.

> — Arthur Miller
> *Death of a Salesman* (1949)

People don't buy what you do; they buy why you do it.

> — Simon Sinek

Are you selling a product, a service, or are you selling yourself? There is a big difference between selling yourself and selling who you are. People do business with people they like and people who understand how they feel. Deciding what you are selling is vital to Rainmaking.

Once you have determined what you are selling, reaffirm *why* you are selling it. You already know that from Strategy #1 — "Discover Your Why". So, you need to know *what* you are selling and *why* you are selling it. Remember what Simon Sinek said: "People don't buy what you do; they buy why you do it."

What are you doing now in your life to impact the world? Why are you doing it?

7 | Know What You're Dealing With

You may think you know what you're dealing with, but, believe me, you don't.

— Noah Cross (John Huston)
Chinatown (1974)

Make sure. Investigate first.

Cautious pilots don't head into a storm blindly. Make sure that you perform your *due diligence*. You must know what you are dealing with.

Knowing what you're dealing with is a tall order. Invest the time to learn everything you can about what you are facing. Knowing what you're dealing with is an ongoing process.

What are you dealing with? What is keeping you from being a Rainmaker today?

8 | Know Who You're Dealing With

You don't want to accept the fact that you're dealing with an expert in guerilla warfare, with a man who's the best, with guns, with knives, with his bare hands. A man who's been trained to ignore pain, ignore weather, to live off the land, to eat things that would make a billy goat puke. In Vietnam, his job was to dispose of enemy personnel. To kill! Period! Win by attrition. Well Rambo was the best.

— Sam Trautman (Richard Crenna)
First Blood (1982)

Don't mess with Rambo.

Make a list of what you think you need to know about WHO you are dealing with.

9 | Lose the 800-pound Gorilla

800-pound gorilla: an overbearing entity in a specific industry or sphere of activity. A seemingly unbeatable presence to be reckoned with . . .

— Urban Dictionary

Negative emotions can kill you. Holding on to negative emotions is like having an 800-pound gorilla on your chest. It will cause you anxiety; and, eventually maybe even a heart attack or a stroke.

You must let go of hatred and resentment. The more that you hold on to them, the more they will grow and the heavier they will get. Someday they will appear right in front of you and crush you. Try alternative methods to deal with negative emotions like Yoga and meditation; or just some great Rainmaking!

Think about the negative emotions that
are suffocating you and what you can do
to **LOSE THE 800-POUND GORILLA.** What
do you need to let go of before you can be
a Rainmaker?

10 | Trust Who You Are

After a while, you learn to ignore the names people call you and just trust who you are.

— Shrek (Mike Myers)
Shrek (2001)

All that matters is how you feel about yourself.

If you are confused about how you feel about yourself, you have a big problem. You must be able to trust yourself.

How do you feel about yourself? Do you trust who you are?

There's more than a "Sticks and Stones" approach. You'll learn to build trust in yourself the same way you learned to walk — one step at a time. Make no mistakes about it, though — unless you believe in who you are, you will never be great Rainmaker.

11 | Stay Focused

Stay focused, go after your dreams and keep moving toward your goals.

— LL Cool J

Like a horse in the Kentucky Derby, think about one thing.

Racehorses wear blinkers to restrict their field of vision and stay focused on what's ahead of them. Stay focused on the finish line.

Think about what distracts you. Are you easily distracted by Facebook, emails, or text messages?

When Forrest was separated from Bubba and ran back to carry him and Lt. Dan to safety, Forrest was focused on one thing and one thing only. There were explosions all around him, and he was dodging bullets (except the one that got him in his butt), but he was focused on one thing: getting his buddies to safety. "Run, Forrest, run!"

STRATEGIES

12 | Create Your Own World

If I had a world of my own, everything would be nonsense. Nothing would be what it is, because everything would be what it isn't. And, contrary wise, what is, it wouldn't be. And, what is wouldn't be, it would. You see?

— Alice
Alice's Adventure in Wonderland
& Through the Looking Glass
Lewis Carroll (1865)

Don't be afraid to create a world of your own. Sometimes the only way you can move forward is to build a world of your own. Make it real!

Make a drawing of Mickey Mouse. When you are finished, write ONE word under it that describes how you feel about the mouse that started it all.

13 | Play the Hand You're Dealt

I needed a drink, I needed a lot of life insurance, I needed a vacation, I needed a home in the country. What I had was a coat, a hat, and a gun. I put them on and went out of the room.

— Raymond Chandler
Farewell My Lovely (1940)

Work with what you have — improvise, if you must. Rainmakers work with what they have.

Make a list of what you must work with at this point in your Rainmaker transformation.

14 | Exorcise Your Demons

Have you ever heard of exorcism? It's a stylized ritual in which rabbis or priests try to drive out the so-called invading spirit. It's pretty much discarded these days, except by the Catholics who keep it in the closet as a sort of embarrassment. It has worked, in fact, although not for the reason they think, of course. It was purely a force of suggestion. The victim's belief in possession helped cause it. And, just in the same way, this belief in the power of exorcism can make it disappear.

— Dr. Barringer (Peter Masterson)
The Exorcist (1973)

We all have demons inside of us and skeletons in our closet.

What demons are lurking in your closet right now? How can you begin to move forward?

You can't worry about the skeletons in your closet. Don't paralyze yourself by giving them any attention, just move forward and make sure you don't collect more.

15 | Surprise Them

You don't understand. I want to be surprised...
astonish me, sport, new info, don't care where or
how you get it, just get it . . .

— Gordon Gekko (Michael Douglas)
Wall Street (1987)

Surprise is a powerful tactic.

Engage people with what they expect; it's what they
can discern and confirms their projections. It settles
them into predictable patterns of response,
occupying their minds while you wait for the
extraordinary moment — that which they cannot
anticipate.

— Sun Tzu
The Art of War

Why do surprises sometimes backfire?

Surprise is a powerful tactic but make sure it doesn't
blow up in your face. You need to be very strategic
about it.

16 | Seduce Them

I appreciate this whole seduction thing you've got going on here, but let me give you a tip: I'm a sure thing.

— Vivian Ward (Julia Roberts)
Pretty Woman (1990)

Come to me, said the spider; to the fly.

When you think about it, life is one big seduction. The trick is to be able to seduce someone without them knowing what you are doing.

Seduction is all about emotions — ALL about emotions. Seduction is the process of using every emotion that you can evoke to get what you want.

Rainmaking is, in its purest form, the process of seduction.

Have you ever been seduced? How did it make you feel?

17 | Finesse Them

As far as I'm concerned, Parnelli Jones was the greatest driver of his era. He had aggressiveness and also finesse that no one else possessed. And he won with everything he put his hands on, including off road.

— Mario Andretti

Parnelli Jones had finesse.

When I was a boy, my father took our family to Ascot Speedway to watch Parnelli Jones race in his Sprint Car (#98). One of the stories that my father enjoyed telling was the one about taking his four kids to watch Parnelli race. He loved telling people that we all knew Parnelli's car number (#98) and that, every time #98 sped by the grandstand, all of us kids would scream "GO PARNELLI!" In 1963 Parnelli won the Indy 500. Parnelli by combining aggressiveness and finesse.

Who in your world has finesse? How do they use it?

There are a lot of words like FINESSE. For Rainmakers, it means having some game — having charisma and the skills to manipulate the situation however you want. Like #98. GO PARNELLI.

18 | Be an Enigma

I cannot forecast to you the action of Russia. It is a riddle wrapped in a mystery, inside an enigma; but perhaps there is a key.

— Winston Churchill

Riddles intrigue people.

I am a businessman. I am anything I need to be at any time.

— Pascal (Ian Holm)
Big Night (1966)

Who is an enigma to you? How do you feel when you are around them?

There are reasons to make yourself a riddle. The main one is to create some mystery about yourself. It should have appeal!

19 | Act as If

Success or failure depends on attitude more than on capacity. Successful men act as though they have accomplished or are enjoying something, soon it becomes reality. Act, look, feel successful, conduct yourself accordingly, and you will be amazed at the positive result.

Attitude is everything.

— William James

She walks like she don't care
Walking on imported air
Ooh, it makes you wanna die

— *Maria* — Blondie
Jimmy Destri (1998)

What does "She walks like she don't care" mean?

20 | Celebrate Your Victories

History remembers KINGS, not soldiers! Tomorrow we'll batter down the gates of Troy. I'll build monuments for victory on every Island of Greece. I'll carve Agamemnon in the stones.

— Agamemnon (Brian Cox)
Troy (2004)

Be generous to yourself.

There are a lot of reasons to celebrate your victories and a lot of ways to celebrate. Be good to yourself — you deserve it.

How do you CELEBRATE YOUR VICTORIES? Make a list of the ways that you are going to celebrate your future achievements.

These are some of the ways that I CELEBRATE MY VICTORIES: Walk on the beach in front of the Montage in Laguna Beach. Enjoy some raw vegan chocolate. Hug my wife and daughter and tell them how much I love them. Light up a Havana Perfecto (just kidding!).

21 | Believe in Angels

When I was a child I thought I saw an angel. It had wings and kinda looked like my sister. I opened the door so some light could come in and it sort of faded away. My mother said it was probably my Guardian Angel.

— Denzel Washington

Each of us has our own Angels.

Do you BELIEVE IN ANGELS? If no, why not?

Do I believe in angels? YES. I believe in God, and I believe in angels. I don't believe in Santa Claus or The Tooth Fairy. I believe in Never-never Land, The Land of Oz, what's down the rabbit hole, what's behind the looking glass, and in Disneyland. I stopped believing in Camelot more than fifty years ago. I don't believe in the words 'natural' or 'organic.' I don't believe in the devil (that's why I didn't capitalize it) and, I don't believe in heaven or hell. I don't believe Macy's when they advertise "20% Off for One Day Only" (especially when they announce the same thing two days later). Getting back to angels: I believe in all kinds of angels.

22 | Just Be Yourself

And rather than hide that, I would rather put that out on the radio and let someone see the full range of emotions. If you're going to be strong on the radio, you got to let it all out, even the ugly stuff. And you can't apologize for it.

— Howard Stern

Being yourself should be easy.

A lot of very successful businessmen share some of these sociopathic traits — a lack of empathy, seeing people as commodities, projecting an air of sincerity when everything is actually calculated.

— Oscar Issac

There's something liberating about not pretending. Dare to embarrass yourself. Risk.

— Drew Barrymore

Listen to Howard Stern for 3 minutes and think about whether he is himself or trying to be someone else.

Many people try to be someone or something they're not. Be yourself, and don't apologize for it.

23 | Make a Grand Entrance

Neither of the two people in the room paid any attention to the way I came in, although only one of them was dead.

— Raymond Chandler
The Big Sleep (1946)

All eyes are always on you.

I like the way you move
I like the way you move (Who!)
I love the way you move
I love the way, I love the way

— *The Way You Move* — OutKast
Big Boi, Carl-Mo, Sleepy Brown (1992)

First impressions are priceless. Always make a grand entrance. Be exactly on time. There is no such thing as being 'fashionably late'.

Think about a time when someone made a negative first impression on you. What made you react the way you did?

24 | Review the Game Tapes

After the game the coach might get the game together to review the game tape. You'll love watching this tape if you played the position and passed accurately and scored whenever you got near the net and got some really good saves. Everyone loves to see himself when they are playing well. It's when you have played lousy that you hate sitting through the game tape.

— J.K. Tinkham
Life Lessons on Ice

Practice your game.

When I started working as a stockbroker, I recorded all my calls on a microcassette recorder. In the evenings, I listened to some of my calls so that I could improve my sales skills.

With today's technology, you can do the same with your smartphone. Practice some of your presentations and always be bettering your skills.

When was the last time you achieved a difficult goal with a phone call? Why did it go so well?

25 | Master Your Moves

Come on, dance
Jump on it
If you sexy then flaunt it
If you freaky then own it
Don't brag about it, come show me
Come on, dance
Jump on it
If you sexy then flaunt it
Well it's Saturday night and we in the spot
Don't believe me just watch (come on)

— *Uptown Funk* — Mark Ronson and Bruno Mars
Jeff Bhasker, Phlip Lawrence, Bruno Mars, Mark Ronson,
Nicholas Williams, Devon Gallaspy, Lonnie Simmons
The Gap Band, Rudolph Taylor (2014)

Move with Power, Grace, and Style.

Body language is important to Rainmakers. Stand tall and don't put your hands in your pockets.

If someone saw you walking down the street, just being yourself, what impression(s) would they form?

The best way to MASTER YOUR MOVES is to learn every Latin dance you can.

26 | Don't Look Too Good

LAW 26 – Never Appear Too Perfect

Appearing better than others is always dangerous, but most dangerous of all is to appear to have no faults or weaknesses. Envy creates silent enemies. It is smart to occasionally display defects, and admit to harmless vices, in order to deflect envy and appear more human and approachable. Only gods and the dead can seem perfect with impunity.

— Robert Greene
The 48 Laws of Power (1998)

There used to be a saying in Colombia about drug dealers who drove Ferraris: "They look like a fly in a glass of milk." At the height of the of the drug war, you would see someone who appeared otherwise insignificant behind the wheel of a new Ferrari. In those times, most people played themselves down because they did not want to call attention to themselves and get kidnapped for ransom.

How do you feel when you are around someone who 'looks too good?'

27 | Get Mad

I want you to get up now and go to the window. Open it, and stick your head out, and yell — 'I'M MAD AS HELL, AND I'M NOT GOING TO TAKE THIS ANYMORE!'

— Howard Beale (Peter Finch)
Network (1976)

Sometimes it's okay to get mad.

Controlled anger can be a good thing. When we get upset about something, we are often moved to take massive action. If the massive action is in our best interest, anger may get us to where we want to be.

Never lose your temper, but never let them think that you are incapable of getting angry. Always be on the edge. The trick is being able to conjure up all the passion of anger to drive you forward, without any of the adverse effects of anger. Anger has driven many people in all directions; forward and backward, up and down. Learn to control your anger and deal with other people's anger.

**When has anger gotten the best of you?
What was the result?**

28 | Don't Be a Hypocrite

If, if a white man puts his arm around me voluntarily, that's brotherhood. But if you — if you hold a gun on him and make him embrace me and pretend to be friendly or brotherly toward me, then that's not brotherhood, that's hypocrisy.

— Malcolm X

Don't be phony.

Think about the phoniest people you know. What habits or behaviors give them away?

29 | Make Your Move

Do it no matter what. If you believe in it, it is something very honorable. If somebody around you or your family does not understand it, then that's their problem. But if you do have a passion, an honest passion, just do it.

— Mario Andretti

A fish that stops moving quickly gets eaten by a shark.

Twenty years from now you will be more disappointed by the things that you didn't do than by the ones you did do. So throw off the bowlines. Sail away from the safe harbor. Catch the trade winds in your sails. Explore. Dream. Discover.

— Mark Twain

Think about it: Where will you be in twenty years?

30 | Keep It Real

Listen, Sherlock. While you were tucked away up here working on your ethics, I was out there busting my hump in the REAL world. And the reason guys like you got a place to teach is 'cause guys like me donate buildings.

— Thorton Melon (Rodney Dangerfield)
Back to School (1986)

Rainmakers make things happen in real ways, in the *real* world.

How can you make an impact in the real world today?

31 | Don't Let Them Fool You

Never be distracted by people's glamorous portraits of themselves and their lives; search and dig for what really imprisons them.

— Robert Greene
The 48 Laws of Power (1998)

Mostly everyone hides behind a façade.

When was the last time someone pretended to be what they were not and fooled you? How did it make you feel?

People like to impress other people. Give them the satisfaction; it costs you absolutely nothing and may do them a lot of good in some inexplicable way. I remember a Beverly Hills attorney, let's call him Bob, who was the real thing. He was a Rainmaker. He knew everybody who was anybody. One day we were having drinks at the Polo Lounge, and he started his usual commentary on the other people there. There was one comment that remains in my mind even today. Bob said: "Look at that guy over there, the one in the leisure suit and the platform shoes. He lives in a one-bedroom apartment in Santa Monica and wants me to believe that he's a dealmaker. I had him checked out. He sells Volvos to doctors during the day, and he wants everyone to think he's another Bernie Cornfeld."

32 | Keep Them Guessing

Benjamin: **For God's sake, Mrs. Robinson. Here we are. You get me into your house. You give me a drink. You...put on music. Now you start opening your personal life to me and tell me your husband won't be home for hours.**

Mrs. Robinson: **So?**

Benjamin: **Mrs. Robinson, you're trying to seduce me.**

Mrs. Robinson: [*laughs*] **Huh?**
Benjamin: **Aren't you?**

> — Benjamin Braddock (Dustin Hoffman)
> Mrs. Robinson (Anne Bancroft)
> *The Graduate* (1967)

Think of a time when you 'showed your hand' and regretted it later. How can you keep from making the same mistake again?

Mystique is one of the greatest techniques. People like mystique. They like to have choices. They like to be able to pick between Door #1, Door #2, and Door #3. Whatever you do, always keep them guessing. Never, never, never show your hand. Once they see your hand, you have lost all your leverage. Never, never, never show your hand.

33 | Create Your Emotional Brand

Your brand is what people say about you when you're not in the room.

— Jeff Bezos

What do people say about you when you're not in the room?

Maybe it's the TV commercials. They make you hate everything they try to sell. God, they must think the public is a halfwit. Every time some jerk in a white coat with a stethoscope hanging around his neck holds up some toothpaste or a pack of cigarettes or a bottle of beer or a mouthwash or a jar of shampoo or a little box of something that makes a fat wrestler smell like mountain lilac, I always make a note never to buy any. Hell, I wouldn't buy the product even if I liked it.

— Raymond Chandler
The Long Goodbye (1953)

How would others describe your
emotional brand?

34 | Be the Expert

Be so good that they can't ignore you.

— Steve Martin

People want to deal with the expert.

What are you an expert in? What do you do or say to show people that you are an expert?

Steve Martin is an expert. He knows how to make people laugh, but there is a role that he played that involved much more than just making people laugh. In *Leap of Faith* (1992), Steve Martin played the leading role of Jonas Nightengale, a charismatic but fraudulent Christian faith healer who traveled across America holding tent revival meetings. Assisted by Jane Larson (Debra Winger), hidden microphones, and people planted in the audience, Martin performed 'miracle' healings. Try to watch *Leap of Faith* and think about how it may, or may not, compare to Rainmaking.

35 | Be a Trusted Advisor

People want to be told what to do so badly that they'll listen to anyone.

— Don Draper (Jon Hamm)
Mad Men (Season 1)

People want to be told what to do.

TRUSTED ADVISOR — two very powerful words. You will discover that once people consider you their trusted advisor, they will ask you for advice on everything from buying a car to planning for retirement.

The operative word, of course, is *trusted*. Anyone can be an advisor; only a select few can be *trusted* advisors.

Who are your trusted advisors? Why do you trust them?

People do business with other people that they like and trust. Above all else in your business relationships, be a TRUSTED ADVISOR.

36 | Be the Product

You are the product. You feeling something. That's what sells. Not them. Not sex. They can't do what we do, and they hate us for it.

> — Don Draper (Jon Hamm)
> *Mad Men* (Season 2)

As usual, no one could have put it better than Don Draper. People buy feelings. YOU ARE THE PRODUCT.

How do you feel about being the product?

37 | Be the First Man

The first man gets the oyster; the second man gets the shell.

— Andrew Carnegie

Always be the first man, or woman, unless you want the shell. If that's the case, you can be the second man or woman.

Always be first in and first out; never first in and last out, and never last in and last out ("Who's on first?").

38 | Be the Second Mouse

Two little mice fell in a bucket of cream. The first mouse quickly gave up and drowned. The second mouse, wouldn't quit. He struggled so hard that he churned that cream into butter and crawled out. Gentlemen, as of this moment, I am the second mouse.

> — Frank Abagnale Sr. (Christopher Walken)
> *Catch Me If You Can* (2002)

Never quit until you're ready.

You just can't beat the person who never gives up.

> — Babe Ruth

Who do you know that never gives up?
How do they make you feel?

39 | Connect

There would have been no Beats deal without the Samsung deal [referring to the deal Jay Z struck with Samsung last year to have his album debut on its phones]. It showed the number one company the importance of connecting with culture.

— Kanye West

Plug into the world around you.

What activities do you do each day to stay connected to the world around you? How do you focus on these activities?

Connecting is the easy part. The challenge is being selective and determining where to focus your energy, especially on social media. Pick two or three and work them hard. I recommend LinkedIn, Facebook, and Twitter.

40 | Disconnect When Necessary

Living off the grid and being kind of an outlaw brings a dangerous reality.

— Ron Perlman

Unplug yourself occasionally. If your smartphone has become a fetish that you can't live without, you have a problem.

Electric communication will never be a substitute for the face of someone who with their soul encourages another person to be brave and true.

— Charles Dickens

Be completely honest: how long could you comfortably go without electronics? A day? A week? A month? A year? Make sure that your smartphone serves you instead of the other way around.

Try going completely OFF the grid one day a week. My day is Sunday. No TV, no emails, and no phone calls or texts (except from my wife, daughter, editor, or Donald Trump).

41 | Pick Your Partners

And when the cops, when they assigned a whole army to stop Jimmy, what'd he do? He made 'em all partners.

— Henry Hill (Ray Liotta)
Goodfellas (1990)

Partners can make or break you.

Who are the best partners you have ever had? What made them so good?

Putting together your team should be a very selective process.

42 | Watch Your Back

My father taught me many things here — he taught me in this room. He taught me: keep your friends close, but your enemies closer.

> — Michael Corleone (Al Pacino)
> *The Godfather: Part II* (1974)

Better to keep your friends close and avoid making enemies.

Who do you trust? How did they earn your trust?

You can never COMPLETELY trust anyone. Never.

43 | Mark Your Turf

If you think psychographically and not demographically, you can really target a lot more audiences.

— Tyra Banks

Target by how people feel, not by who they are.

How big does your world expand? What is your target?

44 | Don't Be Easily Impressed

I had to let it happen, I had to change
Couldn't stay all my life down at heel
Looking out of the window
Staying out of the sun

So, I choose freedom
Running around, trying everything new
But nothing impressed me at all
I never expected it to

> — *Don't Cry for Me Argentina* — Madonna
> Andrew Lloyd Webber and Tim Rice (1976)

She never expected it to. You shouldn't, either.

When was the last time you were easily impressed, only to be disappointed later?

45 | Create Your Visual Style

I don't know about you, but every time some joker points me out as I walk through an airport wearing extra-small Dolfin shorts, a tank top and leg warmers, I get a little upset.

— Richard Simmons

Invent your signature look.

Create your own visual style . . . let it be unique for yourself and yet identifiable for others.

— Oscar Wilde

What is your signature look? How does it differ from others?

Wearing jeans with holes in them made in a Chinese sweatshop is not a signature look. Nor is wearing a cap on backwards — unless you are a baseball catcher. Wearing a doo-rag is a signature look, and so is wearing a bandana on your head. Designer sunglasses, handbags, and printed T-shirts do not create a signature look unless your name is on the logo. Remember, you can put a Tiffany necklace on a pig, and all you will have is a pig with a necklace snorting as it eats a little teal box.

46 | Get on the Cover

We'll, we're big rock singers
We got golden fingers
And were loved everywhere we go... (That sounds like us)
We sing about beauty and we sing about truth
At ten thousand dollars a show . . . (Right)
We take all kinds of pills that give us all kinds of thrills
But the thrill we've never known
Is the thrill that'll getcha when you get your picture
On the cover of the Rollin' Stone

> — *The Cover of Rolling Stone* — Dr. Hook
> Shel Silverstein (1972)

Promote yourself.

What are you currently doing to promote yourself? What else could you be doing?

Get on the cover of *Rolling Stone* and all the other covers that you can. There is no such thing as too much publicity. Even the *National Enquirer* is okay.

47 | Assume Nothing

[*to a woman on the witness stand*]

Ah…you assumed. My dear, you should never
assume. You see, when you assume
[*writes **ass – u - me** on a blackboard*]
. . . you make an ass out of you and me.

— Felix Unger (Tony Randall)
The Odd Couple

**When was the last time you assumed
something, and felt like an ass later?
Would you make the same assumption
today?**

Everyone makes assumptions all the time. Just
watch yourself and don't make an ASS out of
yourself.

48 | Imagine

Disneyland will never be completed. It will continue to grow as long as there is imagination left in the world.

— Walt Disney

Imagine — it all started with a mouse.

Mickey Mouse popped out of my mind onto a drawing pad 20 years ago on a train ride from Manhattan to Hollywood at a time when business fortunes of my brother Roy and myself were at lowest ebb and disaster seemed right around the corner.

— Walt Disney

Think about how you feel when you hear those six magical letters: DISNEY.

49 | Never Let Them See You Sweat

Never let them see you sweat.

— Gillette Companies

When people believe they've gotten to you, you're done!

How many times have you heard this slogan without thinking about what it means for a Rainmaker? What do you do to stay calm when things get tough?

50 | Self-correct

If one dream dies, dream another dream. If you get knocked down, get back up and go again.

— Joel Osteen

Program yourself to self-correct. Engage autopilot.

Analyze and correct your past mistakes before they paralyze your future. An undiscovered error will always crave for repetition. Kick out errors; enjoy a bright future.

— Israeimore Ayivor

Think about a serious mistake that you have made. What did you learn from it?

51 | Perfect Your Timing

The first cut is the deepest, baby, I know
The first cut is the deepest

— The First Cut is the Deepest — Cat Stevens
Cat Stevens (1967)

Always be first in and last out, and remember:
"the first cut is the deepest."

Focus on something that is happening in
the world today that makes you angry.
What you do to begin to work for positive
change, today?

52 | Don't Be Surprised When You Lose

You have no choices about how you lose, but you do have a choice about how you come back and prepare to win again.

— Pat Riley

Losing is a risk of trying.

Nobody wants to lose. How do you feel about losing?

53 | Turn Yourself Into Your Customer

If you can't turn yourself into your customer, you probably shouldn't be in the ad business.

— Leo Burnett

Trade places.

**Would you make a deal with yourself?
Why or why not?**

54 | Keep Your Customer Satisfied

And it's the same old story
Everywhere I go
I get slandered, libeled
I hear words I never heard in the Bible
And I'm so tired
I'm oh, so tired
But I'm trying to keep my customers satisfied
Satisfied

— *Keep the Customer Satisfied* — Paul Simon
Paul Simon (1969)

Just don't be patronizing.

It is so much easier to be nice, to be respectful, to put yourself in your customers' shoes and try to understand them before they ask for help than it is to try to mend a broken relationship.

— Mark Cuban

Think about a time when you were a satisfied customer. What made you feel that way?

There is a difference, a BIG difference between keeping them satisfied and kissing their asses.

55 | Let's Go Crazy

So when you call that shrink up in Beverly Hills
You know the one — Dr. Everything'll Be Alright
Instead of asking him how much of your time is left
Ask him how much of your mind, baby

> — *Let's Go Crazy* — Prince
> Prince Nelson (1984)

Party like it's 1999.

The only people for me are the mad ones, the ones
who are mad to live, mad to talk, mad to be saved,
desirous of everything at the same time, the ones
who never yawn or say a commonplace thing, but
burn, burn, burn, like fabulous yellow roman candles
exploding like spiders across the stars and in the
middle you see the blue center light pop and
everybody goes "Aww!"

> — Jack Kerouac

Listen to *Let's Go Crazy* by Prince. How
does it make you feel? When was the last
time you went crazy?

56 | Live Like There's No Tomorrow

'Cause I've lost loved ones in my life
Who never new how much I loved them
Now I live with the regret
That my true feelings for them never were revealed

— If Tomorrow Never Comes — Garth Brooks
Garth Brooks and Kent Blazy (1988)

What if tomorrow never comes?

Don't count the days. Make the days count.

— Muhammad Ali

Dance like there's nobody watching.
Love like you'll never be hurt.
Sing like there's nobody listening.
And live like it's heaven on earth.

— William W. Purkey

Make each day your masterpiece.

— John Wooden

**What day in your life has been your
masterpiece so far? What made it so?**

57 | Always Have One More Thing

There's just one more thing, sir!

> — Lt. Columbo (Peter Falk)
> *Prescription: Murder* (1968)

Without being as annoying as Columbo, always have one more thing.

There are a couple of loose ends I'd like to tie up. Nothing important you understand.

> — Lt. Columbo (Peter Falk)
> *Dead Weight* (1971)

When in your life have you wished that you had taken the time to find out one more thing? What would that one more thing have been, and how would it have made a difference?

58 | Know When to Fold 'Em

You've got to know when to hold 'em
Know when to fold 'em
Know when to walk away
And know when to run

> — *The Gambler* — Kenny Rogers
> Don Schlitz (1978)

Sometimes it's just time to quit.

Think of a time in your life when you should have quit, but didn't. What were the short-term and long-term effects? What did you learn?

59 | Show Some Class

My dear girl, there are some things that just aren't done. Such as Drinking Dom Perignon '53 above the temperature of 38 degrees Fahrenheit. That's just as bad as listening to the Beatles without earmuffs.

— James Bond (Sean Connery)
Goldfinger (1964)

Shaken, not stirred.

Who do you know that has real class?
What effect does their class have on the people around them?

Remember that flash is not CLASS. Class is intrinsic. You can't buy class, and you can't obtain it with designer brands. Class has more to do with how you act than how you look.

60 | Be Extraordinary

The thing about Hitchcock which is quite extraordinary for a director of that time, he had a very strong sense of his own image and publicizing himself. Just a very strong sense of himself as the character of Hitchcock.

— Toby Jones

Defy the ordinary.

Love yourself first and everything else falls into life. You have to love yourself to get anything done in this world.

— Lucille Ball

What is extraordinary about you? Do not proceed to the next strategy until you have an answer.

Being extraordinary often just means being yourself.

61 | Supersize Your Dreams

I started out mopping the floor just like you guys. But now . . . now I'm washing lettuce. Soon I'll be on fries; then the grill. And pretty soon, I'll make assistant manager, and that's when the big bucks start rolling in.

> — Maurice (Louie Anderson)
> *Coming to America* (1988)

Go BIG.

You are never too old to set another goal or dream a new dream.

> — C.S. Lewis

What is your biggest dream? Say it out loud or write it down and then GO FOR IT.

If you think that you can be the assistant manager, you might as well set your sights on being the owner. Go BIG!

62 | Sell Them Their Dreams

'Sell them their dreams,' a woman radio announcer urged a convention of display men in 1923. 'Sell them what they longed for and hoped for and almost despaired of having. Sell them hats by splashing sunlight across them. Sell them dreams — dreams of country clubs and proms and visions of what might happen if only. After all, people don't buy things to have things. They buy things to work for them. They buy hope — hope of what your merchandise will do for them. Sell them this hope and you won't have to worry about selling them goods.'

— William R. Leach
Land of Desire

Didn't you love the things that they stood for?
Didn't they try to find some good for you and me?
And we'll be free
Someday soon, it's gonna be one day

Anybody here seen my old friend Bobby?
Can you tell me where he's gone?
I thought I saw him walkin' up over the hill
With Abraham, Martin and John

— *Abraham, Martin and John* — Dion
Dick Holler (1968)

**Who in your life has made you feel like
your dreams are possible? How did it
make you feel to have them say so?**

63 | Know What You're Worth

Well, first of all, I'm worth every penny.

— Howard Stern

If you are good at what you do, charge well for it.

The cost of a thing is the amount of what I call life which is required to be exchanged for it.

— Henry David Thoreau

What talents might you cultivate in yourself to be worth as much as Howard Stern?

64 | Be Consistent

Everybody says one thing and then does another.

— Nicole Walker (Reese Witherspoon)
Fear (1996)

If you talk the talk, walk the walk.

How do you feel about people whose words and actions are inconsistent?

65 | Develop Street Smarts

I was street smart, but unfortunately the street was Rodeo Drive.

— Carrie Fisher

Being street smart is not about where you went to college — it's about where you live and work, and how well you can make RAIN there.

How important is being STREET SMART to your business or profession? To you personally?

66 | Earn Street Cred

As far as my street cred goes, I'll always have that because I always hang with the kids. I'll jump right off the stage and buy them a beer. I'll be a star on stage, but I'll always hang with the kids.

— Kid Rock

Get them to respect you. Respect is the one thing that must be earned. There is no other way to get it.

Who has earned your respect? Why did you give it to them?

67 | Make Friends in Low Places

I'm not big on social graces
Think I'll slip down to the Oasis
Oh, I've got friends in low places

> — *Friends in Low Places* — Garth Brooks
> Dewayne Blackwell and Earl Bud Lee (1989)

Don't be a snob.

I can relate to anyone. I can hang out with stoners, skaters, surfers, stockbrokers, lawyers, athletes, rappers. I can hang out with any group of people and find common ground to talk with them.

> —Barry Zito

When was the last time you behaved as if associating with someone else was beneath you? What does it feel like to be treated that way?

68 | Get Money for Nothin'

And he's up there, what's that? Hawaiian noises?
You bangin' on the bongos like a chimpanzee
Oh that ain't workin' that's the way you do it
Get your money for nothin' get your chicks for free

> — *Money for Nothing* — Dire Straits
> Mark Knopfler and Sting (1994)

Work smart, so you don't have to work so hard.

I want money
I want lots of money
In fact, I want so much money
Give me your money
Just give me money

> — *Money (That's What I Want)* — Flying Lizards
> Barry Gordy and Janie Bradford (1959)

Hip-hop deals with bragging and braggadocio, being boastful. It's always been about who's got the most money.

> — Two Chainz

Listen to Dire Straits singing *Money for Nothing*. Better yet, grab your air microphone and sing along!

69 | Have No Fear

Sometimes, it's not so easy being Fearless Leader.

— Fearless Leader (Robert De Niro)
The Adventures of Rocky & Bullwinkle (2000)

Fear is all in your mind.

Make a list of your top ten fears. You don't need the scientific names. What is the first step you might take to conquer each one?

70 | Do It Your Way

For what is a man, what has he got
If not himself, then he is naught
To say the words he truly feels
And not the words of one who kneels
The record shows I took my blows
And did it my way

— *My Way* — Frank Sinatra
Paul Anka (1969)

The Chairman of the Board says it all.

You'll learn, as you get older, that rules are made to be broken. Be bold enough to live life on your terms, and never, ever apologize for it. Go against the grain, refuse to conform, take the road less travelled instead of the well-beaten path. Laugh in the face of adversity, and leap before you look. Dance as though EVERYBODY is watching. March to the beat of your own drummer. And, stubbornly refuse to fit in.

— Mandy Hale
The Single Woman: Life, Love, and a Dash of Sass

What was the last thing you did purely to express yourself? How did it make you feel?

71 | Don't Be a Bully

[*successful lobbyist for Big Tobacco addressing middle-school students at a Career Day speech*]

Kid #3: **My Mommy says smoking kills.**

Mike Naylor: **Oh, is your Mommy a doctor?**

Kid #3: **No.**

Mike Naylor: **A scientific researcher of some kind?**

Kid #3: **No.**

Mike Naylor: **Well, then she's hardly a credible expert, is she?**

— Nick Naylor (Aaron Eckhart)
Thank You for Not Smoking (2006)

You can always find midgets.

In any circus, you can always find midgets.

— David Chase (Edmund Lowe)
Front Page Detective
Murder Rides the Night Train (1951)

When was the last time anyone purposefully made you feel small or weak? How can you avoid doing this yourself?

72 | Ask

Most people never pick up the phone, most people never ask. And that's what separates, sometimes, the people that do things from the people that just dream about them. You gotta act. And you gotta be willing to fail. If you're afraid of failing, you won't get very far.

— Steve Jobs

Ask for the order!

When was the last time you missed out on something because you did not ask for what you wanted? How did you feel afterwards?

Don't be afraid to ask for the order — again and again.

73 | Stay Fly

I believe that my clothes can give people a better image of themselves — that they can increase their feelings of confidence and happiness.

— Georgio Armani

Dress to impress.

I care deeply about the half-time show, deeply. I got dressed for the half-time show. I hope Beyoncé likes what I have on.

— Barack Obama

When was the last time you were under-dressed for an occasion? How did it make you feel?

There's a difference, a big difference, between J.C. Penney and Georgio Armani. Know what to wear, when.

74 | Look in the Mirror

Go home, take a paper bag and cut some eyeholes out of it. Put it over your head, get undressed and look at yourself in the mirror. Really evaluate where your strengths and weaknesses are. And be honest.

— Joan Holloway (Christina Hendricks)
Mad Men (Season 1)

Mirror, mirror on the wall...

What parts of yourself are you least comfortable to look at, and why?

You don't need to look into the mirror . . . just look into your soul.

75 | Manage Your Reputation

Your brand name is only as good as your reputation.

— Richard Branson

Don't get a bad rep.

Think of three celebrated people whose reputations were damaged, only to result in them becoming more celebrated later.

Don't get upset if you see your picture on the cover of the *National Enquirer* with a story about you having sex with aliens.

76 | Take Risks

The biggest risk is not taking any risk . . . In a world that's changing really quickly, the only strategy that is guaranteed to fail is not taking risks.

— Mark Zuckerberg

You'll always miss 100% of the shots you don't take.

— Wayne Gretzky

Take calculated risks. That is quite different from being rash.

— General George S. Patton

Make a list of three risks you have taken that worked out well for you OR make a list of three risks you wish you had taken. Which list is easier for you to complete and WHY?

77 | Help the Elephant

There's a phrase, 'the elephant in the living room,' which purports to describe what it is like to live with a drug addict, an alcoholic, an abuser. People outside such relationships will sometimes ask, 'How could you let such a business go on for so many years? And, it's so hard for anyone living in a more normal situation to understand the answer that comes closer to the truth: 'I'm sorry but it was there when I moved in. I didn't know it was an elephant, I thought it was part of the furniture.' There comes an aha-moment for some folks — the lucky ones — when they suddenly recognize the difference.

— Stephen King

Help the elephant get out of the living room.

What is the **ELEPHANT** in your living room? How does it hold you back?

78 | Get Them to Drink Your Kool-Aid

. . . There was one man who became completely withdrawn . . . I want to say catatonic, because we tried to bring him out of it, and could not make contact at all . . . he was sort of a friend of mine, and I had some responsibility for getting him back to town . . . he had a previous history of mental hospitals, lack of contact with reality, etc., and when I realized what had happened, I begged him not to drink the Kool-Aid, but he did . . . and it was very bad.

— Tom Wolfe
The Electric Kool-Aid Acid Test

In the final analysis, you can't FORCE anyone to do anything — you need to use *the power of persuasion.* You must think of a way to emotionally attract people to you and what you are offering. You must get them to *believe* in you. You must get them to drink your Kool-Aid.

What does it take for you to get 'in the zone?' How do you get others to 'get in the zone' and stay there?

79 | Save the Cheap Sales Talk

Save the cheap salesman talk, will ya, it's obvious.

— Gordon Gekko (Michael Douglas)
Wall Street (1987)

Our business is infested with idiots who try to impress by using pretentious jargon.

— David Ogilvy

So many salespeople sound like salespeople. The best thing to do is to be yourself — be natural.

Make a video of yourself, pay attention to what you are saying and how you are saying it.

You may be unintentionally doing or saying things without realizing that you are You may think that you have been trained to be a great salesperson. But, you might be using terms like 'no brainer' and 'earn your business'. And, how many times do you say 'actually'?

80 | Don't Talk Smack

I was a bouncer for nine years, it was all I knew how to do, and my training was not to talk loosely . . . That's still my thought process: Shut your mouth, watch your back and keep working till your ass falls off.

— Vin Diesel

Rainmakers don't talk smack.

Don't put yourself down and don't put other people down. If you want to talk about someone, be positive!

Think about the last time you heard someone 'talking smack'. How did it affect your level of respect for that person?

81 | Play

Life moves pretty fast. You don't stop and look around once in a while, you could miss it.

— Ferris Bueller (Matthew Broderick)
Ferris Bueller's Day Off (1986)

Ferris is a GREAT role model.

When was the last time you took the time
to play? How did it make you feel?

82 | Pray

Pray to whomever, whatever, and whenever you choose. Pray to the mountain, pray to the ancestors, pray to the Earth, pray to the Tao (but it won't listen!), pray to the Great Mother, pray to Jehovah, Allah, Buddha, Jesus, Lakshmi, Siva, pray to the Great Spirit, it makes no difference. Praying is merely a device for realigning the mind, energy, and passion of your universal self. When you pray, you are praying to the god or goddess within you. This has an effect on your energy field, which in turn translates into a positive change that makes something good happen.

— Stephen Russell
Barefoot Doctor's Guide to the Tao
A Spiritual Handbook for the Urban Warrior

What force or deity fills you with awe?
Take a minute to pray for positive change.

83 | Stop Pleasing Others

Alice, you cannot live your life to please others. The choice must be yours because when you step out to face that creature, you will step out alone.

— White Queen (Anne Hathaway)
Alice in Wonderland (2010)

How do you spell doormat? There is a difference between being a 'pleaser' and being a Rainmaker. Rainmakers are not pleasers. Rainmakers do not live their lives to please others.

What happened the last time you tried to please everyone? How did you feel when you were done?

The White Queen is right: "You cannot live your life to please others."

84 | Stop Following Rules

You don't learn to walk by following rules. You learn to walk by doing, and by falling over.

— Richard Branson

Rainmakers are innovators!

Think about a time in your life when you decided to ditch the rules and do something your way. How did you learn more about yourself in the process?

85 | Be a Cinderella Story

Cinderella story. Outta nowhere. A former greenskeeper, now, about to become the Masters champion. It looks a miracle . . . It's in the hole! It's in the hole! It's in the hole!

— Carl Spackler (Bill Murray)
Caddyshack (1980)

Make yourself a legend in their minds.

What is the difference between being confident and bragging? Which one best describes you today?

86 | Reinvent Yourself Daily

There's nothing more addictive or incredible in life than reinventing yourself and allow yourself to be different every day.

—Thalia

I'm feeling good from my head to my shoes
Know where I'm going and I know what to do
I tidied it up my point of view
I got a new attitude.

— *New Attitude* — Patti LaBelle
Sharon Teresa Robinson (1984)

When things are bad, it's the best time to reinvent yourself.

— George Lopez

Wake up each day a new Super Mega-Rainmaker.

If you could change three things about yourself right now, what would you choose and WHY?

87 | Look for the Next Cow

I don't like looking back. I'm always constantly looking forward. I'm not the one to sit and cry over spilt milk. I'm too busy looking for the next cow.

— Gordon Ramsey

Always look for the next cow.

Watch a Gordon Ramsey video and notice how everyone follows his directions without questioning: "Yes, Chef." They all want to be the next cow!

88 | Be Where the Puck Is Going

I skate to where the puck is going to be, not where it has been.

— Wayne Gretzky

Develop a sixth sense.

Think about a time when you followed your intuition to achieve success. What made you listen to the voice within?

As a financial advisor, I have probably told the story of Wayne Gretzky and the puck 1,000 times or more.

89 | Don't Underestimate or Overestimate

Don't underestimate your opponent, but don't overestimate them, either.

— Nancy Pelosi

Everyone in the world has one area of expertise, however large or small it may be, about which he or she knows more than you ever will. Rainmakers learn to recognize and learn from the strengths of those with whom they interact.

Think about a time when you underestimated or overestimated someone and failed to achieve a goal or close a deal thus. How can you avoid making the same mistake again?

90 | Help Them With the Math

One of the most amazing things about mathematics is the people who do math aren't usually interested in application, because mathematics itself is truly a beautiful art form. It's structures and patterns, and that's what we love, and that's what we get off on.

— Danica McKellar

There is probably not much worse than not knowing the numbers of your deal. Know the numbers inside and out. Know them forward and backward. Know them in your sleep. When that moment comes, and it will, when someone says that they are confused about the numbers, that's when you jump in, look around, smile, and confidently say: "Let me help you with the math."

When have you come out on the losing end of a situation by not knowing the numbers inside and out? How can you avoid being in that position again?

91 | Create Hype, Don't Ever Believe It

My own saying is: 'Create the hype, but don't ever believe it.'

— Simon Cowell

We are smothered by hype.

What do you think about Simon Cowell's saying: "Create the hype, but don't ever believe it."

92 | Push! Push! Push!

There's no such thing as too far. You understand? You push everything as far as you can. You push and you push until it starts pushing back. And then you push some goddamn more.

— Walter Abrams (Al Pacino)
Two for The Money (2005)

Push until you get what you want.

What do you want? Who do you want it from? How will you push hard enough without pushing too hard?

93 | Make an Offer They Can't Refuse

Michael Corleone: **My father made him an offer he couldn't refuse.**

Kay Adams: **What was that?**

Michael Corleone: **Luca Brasi held a gun to his head, and my father assured him that either his brains or his signature would be on the contract.**

Kay Adams: . . .

Michael Corleone: . . . **That's a true story.**

— *The Godfather* (1972)

There's always an offer they can't refuse.

When was the last time someone made you an offer you couldn't refuse? What did you learn from the experience?

94 | Get Their Money Now

Only one thing counts in this world: Get them to sign on the line that is dotted.

— Blake (Alec Baldwin)
Glengarry Glen Ross (1992)

Look, I ain't in this for your revolution, and I'm not in it for you, princess. I expect to be well paid. I'm in it for the money.

— Han Solo (Harrison Ford)
Star Wars Episode IV (1977)

Always live by the 'Call Girl Principle' — expect to be paid; moreover, expect to paid what you are worth.

How much are you worth? Find out how much it would cost you to hire someone to do what you are doing. Remember that number.

95 | Don't Buy Into Drama

There comes a time in your life, when you walk away from all the drama and people who create it. You surround yourself with people who make you laugh. Forget the bad and focus on the good. Love the people who treat you right, pray for the ones who do not. Life is too short to be anything but happy. Falling down is a part of life, getting back up is living.

— José N. Harris

Drama is for sitcoms.

Think about the last major drama that got in your way. How did you feel?

96 | Save Your Best Play for Last

Fellas . . . I don't recognize the right of this committee to ask me these kinds of questions. And, furthermore, you can all go fuck yourselves.

— Howard Prince (Woody Allen)
The Front (1976)

Always have an Ace up your sleeve, or even a Joker. This one is simple. Never show all your cards up front. Always be playing your best. But, save your best play for last.

Think about the last time someone played you by playing an 'ace' or a 'joker.' What did you take away from the experience?

97 | Avoid Trouble

Hey, Tony. Remember what I told you when you first started working for me, the guys that last in this business are the guys who fly straight. Low-key, quiet. But the guys who want it all, chicas, champagne, flash . . . they don't last.

— Frank Lopez (Robert Loggia)
Scarface (1983)

And stay out of jail.

What is the difference between bending the rules and breaking the law? How far will you go to get what you want? If getting what you want involves going too far, you might be going after the wrong things.

98 | Flirt With Danger

The danger? Well, of course. But you are missing a very important point. I think if any of us imagined — really imagined — what it would be like to go into a tree at 150 miles per hour we would probably never get into the cars at all, none of us. So it always seemed to me that to do something very dangerous requires a certain absence of imagination.

— Jean-Pierre Sarti (Yves Montand)
Grand Prix (1966)

If things seem under control, you are just not going fast enough.

— Mario Andretti

Look danger in the eye and smile at it.

Do you challenge yourself to face your fears? If not, why not?

99 | Speak the Truth

It does not require many words to speak the truth.

— Chief Joseph
Nez Pierce Tribe

Never lie, it's not worth it.

What was the last lie you told? How did it make you feel to have to live the lie once you told it?

100 | Color Outside the Lines

You can't use up creativity. The more you use, the more you have.

— Maya Angelou

Sometimes I feel like I have been coloring outside the lines my entire life. Color outside the lines, every chance you get — or, forget about the coloring book and draw freehand.

Draw and a picture of something you want. How many details can you include? Rainmakers focus on what they want.

It's not just about coloring outside the lines. Think outside the lines. Feel outside the lines. Live outside the lines. A few weeks ago, our daughter Ali mentioned that I always 'color outside the lines.' Thanks, Ali, for Strategy #100.

101 | Come Right to the Point

Izo Yamura: **In the war, I was a fighter pilot. I shot down 17 American planes.**

Pete Aron: **Okay.**

Izo Yamura: **I believe that some things must not be left unsaid. There will come a time when you will ask yourself, 'What did he do in the war, this man, Yamura?'**

Pete Aron: **Mr. Yamura, I like you.**

Izo Yamura: **Why?**

Pete Aron: **Well, because . . . because you come right to the point.**

Izo Yamura: **In a sense, you are here because you drive a car the way I conduct my business. You come right to the point.**

> — Pete Aron (James Garner)
> Izo Yamura (Toshiro Mifune)
> *Grand Prix* (1966)

Skip the small talk.

Write down one of your deal-making conversations from memory and then restate your entire half of the conversation in fewer than 25 words.

102 | Solicit Feedback

I think it's important to have a feedback loop, where you're constantly thinking about what you've done and how you could be doing it better.

— Elon Musk

Never hesitate to ask how you're doing, even if you know.

> Think of a time when you would have done better if you had asked for feedback. Write down what you imagine the feedback would have been if you had asked.

And, when you ask for feedback, ask people how they *feel* besides asking them what they think.

103 | Enjoy the Ride

It's not about what happened in the past, or what you think might happen in the future. It's about the ride, for Christ's sake. There is no point in going through all this crap, if you are not going to enjoy the ride. And you know what . . .when you least expect something great might come along. Sometime better then you ever planned for.

— Irving Feffer (Bob Dishy)
Along Came Polly (2004)

Make every ride an E-ticket.

Ever been to Disneyland? That was definitely an E-ticket.

— Sally Ride

Do something magical and fun and enjoy every minute of it. Allow yourself to be enchanted.

104 | Reflect

[*voiceover*]

Saigon . . . shit; I'm still only in Saigon . . . 'Every time I think I'm gonna wake up back in the jungle. When I was home after my first tour, it was worse.
[*grabs at flying insect*]
I'd wake up, and there'd be nothing. I hardly said a word to my wife, until I said 'yes' to a divorce. When I was there, all I could think about was getting back to the jungle. I'm here a week now . . . waiting for a mission . . . getting softer. Every minute I stay in this room, I get weaker, and every minute Charlie squats in the bush, he gets stronger. Each time I looked around the walls moved in a little tighter.

> — Captain Benjamin L. Willard (Martin Sheen)
> *Apocalypse Now* [opening scene] (1979)

Always know where you are. Reflection is a reality check. It's different than a stroll down Memory Lane. Why do we glance in our rear-view mirrors while we are driving?

Reflect upon a time when you tried and failed. What would you differently if you could relive the experience today?

105 | Never Say You're Sorry

My wife heard me say I love you a thousand times, but she never once heard me say sorry.

— Bruce Willis

Apologies make you appear weak. Sorry is only a word; but a weak word. And, most words mean nothing without action. Actions are what matters. If you want to turn someone around, saying you're sorry doesn't matter. What's important is what you do. Never say you're sorry. Just act to fix the problem.

Think about a time in your life when you apologized without acting when action might have saved the day. What action could you have taken?

106 | Never Appear Desperate

Rock 'n Roll. The most brutal, ugly, desperate, vicious form of expression it has been my misfortune to hear.

— Frank Sinatra

Desperate people are scary. Beggars appear desperate; don't be a beggar. Desperation scares people and makes them run away and avoid you. Too many phone calls, voice messages, text messages, and emails are all signs of desperation. Play it cool. Throw out the bait and wait for them to come to you. The operative word is 'wait.' Be patient. Never appear desperate.

Think about a time when you might have achieved success if you had just been patient. What might you have done differently?

107 | Call Attention to Yourself

Unless you call attention to your presence, who will know you're there? Even a country has to weave and wave a flag as proof of existence.

— Rod McKuen

Improvisation works.

Put yourself in a familiar situation and behave differently. Keep trying until positive change starts to happen. That's Rainmaking!

108 | Learn to Act

Now Ann, in this one, you're looking down. When I start to crank, you look up slowly. You're quite calm. You don't expect to see a thing. Then, you just follow my instructions. All right? Camera. [*Denham starts cranking.*] Look up slowly, Ann. That's it. You don't see anything. Now look higher. Still higher. Now you see it. You're amazed! You can't believe it. Your eyes open wider. It's horrible, Ann, but you can't look away. There's no chance for you, Ann. No escape. You're helpless, Ann, helpless. There's just one chance, if you can scream. But your throat's paralyzed. Try to scream, Ann. Try. Perhaps if you didn't see it, you could scream. Throw your arms across your eyes and scream, Ann, scream for your life!

[*Ann lets loose a blood-curdling, ear-piercing shrieking scream into the wind.*]

— Carl Denham (Robert Armstrong)
King Kong (1933)

Act . . . *Well*.

Pick your favorite quote from this book
and practice saying it aloud as
expressively as you can. Record yourself
and don't stop until you believe yourself.

109 | Be the Last Coca-Cola

Anna Maria: **He thinks he's the last Coca-Cola in the desert.**
Lanna Lake: **Honey, he is.**

— Anna Maria (Cordella González)
Lanna Lake (Cathy Moriarty)
Mambo Kings (1992)

Make **them believe you're special by making them special.** Make people believe you are special. And, make them feel that they are special because you are working with them. People should feel fortunate to have you. Be the last Coca-Cola in the desert.

Think about the people who make you feel that they are special. What do they do to make you feel that way?

110 | Be Exclusive

You want to know how to get people to trust you with their money? I'll tell you right now. You present it as an exclusive thing . . . Nothing on Earth makes people want something more than telling them they can't have it.

— Bernard Madoff (Richard Dreyfus)
Madoff (2015)

To avoid being mistaken for a sellout, I chose my friends carefully. The more politically active black students. The Marxist professors and structural feminists and punk-rock performance poets.

— Barack Obama

Make them *feel* they're special. Tell them they can't have it and they'll want it even more. It's human nature. People don't like to be told no. You don't need to lie, but you can play hard to get.

How do you make them feel they're special?

111 | Don't Wear No Stinkin' Badges

Badges, to god-damned hell with badges! We have no badges. In fact, we don't need badges. I don't have to show you any stinking badges, you god-damned *cabron* and *chinga tu madre*!

— B. Travern
The Treasure of the Sierra Madre (1927)

Make them remember your name and face — not your badge. I never wear a badge. Why? Because I want people to remember my name and face.

The next time you wear a badge at a networking event, pay attention to how many people scan your badge with their eyes before establishing eye contact with you.

112 | Don't Screw the Pooch

Gordon Cooper: You know something, Gus? I got me a new house, new furniture. Got me a $25,000 a year magazine contract. Got me a Corvette. Got free lunch from one end of America to the other — and I ain't even been up there yet.

Gus Grissom: Yeah, I noticed that.

Gordon Cooper: Oh, you noticed that, did you? Well, I guess they're just saving the best for last.

Gus Grissom: Yeah, I guess so, Hot Dog. Just be sure you don't screw the pooch.

— Gordon Cooper (Dennis Quaid)
Gus Grissom (Fred Ward)
The Right Stuff (1983)

Normally, it takes years to work your way up to the twenty-seventh floor. But it only takes 30 seconds to be out on the street again. You dig?

— J.D. Sheldrake (Fred MacMurray)
The Apartment (1960)

When have you screwed the pooch? What could you have done differently?

113 | Hit Hard, Hit Fast, Hit Often

Hit hard, hit fast, hit often.

— Lt. General Lewis "Chesty" Puller
The United States Marine Corps

And hit 'em where it hurts! Once you let someone get the jump on you, you're done. Be the fastest horse out of the gate. Start out in the lead and stay in the lead until you win.

When have you lost an opportunity because you waited too long? Why did you wait?

114 | Don't Oversell

You had me at hello.

> — Dorothy Boyd (Renee Zellweger)
> *Jerry Maguire* (1996)

Know when to stop talking. Most salespeople don't know when to shut up. They are anxious to impress people with their product knowledge or convince them to but something. So, they just keep talking and talking and talking.

Rainmaking is all about timing. It's about knowing what to say and when to say it. Most important, it's about listening.

Don't oversell. Know when to stop talking. You probably had them at 'hello.'

When have you oversold something, and lost out? What caused you to make that mistake?

115 | Leave 'Em Laughing

Hey, didja hear that? We're competing with Archie and Jughead!

— Gus Grissom (Fred Ward)
The Right Stuff (1983)

You don't have to be a clown to make people laugh.

A horse walks into a bar, and the bartender asks: "Why the long face?"

That stupid joke makes me crack up. Sometimes, the sillier jokes are, the more people laugh at them. Laughter is contagious. Always leave them laughing.

Do an internet search for 'silly jokes,' pick your favorite one, and learn it.

116 | Don't Be Too Serious

It's nice people can finally loosen up a little bit and just go out laugh at silliness. I mean, people take themselves way too seriously sometimes.

— Larry the Cable Guy

Laugh at your life, sometimes. Don't be too serious. When you find yourself stressed, look at yourself in the mirror and try not to laugh. Within a few minutes, you are sure to start cracking up.

If you have the guts, try this trick when someone is mad. Hold up a small mirror so that they can see their reflection. They will try not to look in the mirror. Within minutes, maybe seconds, they will look into the mirror and then start laughing.

Try the mirror trick on yourself. It works!

117 | Speak English

The governor of Texas, who, when asked if the Bible should be taught in Spanish, replied that 'if English was good enough for Jesus, then it's good enough for me.'

— Christopher Hitchens

English is the language of business; or is it?

Translate: *Totó, me parace que ya no estamos en Kansas.*

118 | Learn a Second Language

If you talk to a man in a language he understands, that goes to his head. If you talk to him in his own language, that goes to his heart.

— Nelson Mandela

Are YOU talking to me? There are three sure-fire ways to learn a second language: (1) Get involved romantically with someone who speaks the language you want to learn. (2) Spend a year in a foreign country where the official language is the one you want to learn. (3) Rosetta Stone.

Almost everyone you will deal with will probably speak English. But, speaking people's native language to them has big advantages.

Pick a language, look up the words for three common things you use every day, and learn them.

119 | Don't Let Them Trick You

When success comes, people can try to trick you or take advantage of you.

— Christina Aguilera

When our emotions are engaged, we often have trouble seeing things as they are.

— Robert Greene
The Art of Seduction

Don't fall for anything out of Felix the Cat's Magic Bag of Tricks.

Think about the last trick you fell for. Why did it fool you?

120 | Don't Put Them in a Trick Bag

Tricks and treachery are the practice of fools that don't have enough brains to be honest.

— Benjamin Franklin

Refrain from abusing your magical powers.

Have you ever tried to put someone in a trick bag? What happened and how did they feel? How did you feel?

121 | Don't Let Them Wear You Down

Somewhere along the line we stopped believing we could do anything. And if we don't have our dreams, we have nothing.

— Charles Farmer (Billy Bob Thornton)
The Astronaut Farmer (2006)

Don't be your own worst enemy.

Think about a time when you sabotaged yourself. Why did you do it? What went wrong?

122 | Live Raw and Unplugged

Rollin' down the Imperial Highway
With a big nasty redhead at my side
Santa Ana winds blowin' hot from the north
And we was born to ride

Roll down the window
Crank up the Beach Boys, baby
Don't let the music stop
We're gonna ride it till we just can't ride it no more

— *I Love L.A.* — Randy Newman
Randy Newman (1983)

Big Nasty Redhead?

The Mamas and The Papas sang: "You gotta go where you wanna go, do what you wanna do with who you wanna do it with."

In 1968 Nike launched their highly successful JUST DO IT! Campaign.

Do something you have wanted to do for a long time.

123 | Build Your Network

The key to this business is personal relationships.

— Dickey Fox (Jared Jussim)
Jerry Maguire (1996)

Build a proprietary network of the best and the brightest.

Make a list of at least five people you know right now who would be good to have in your network. Ask them.

Building **YOUR NETWORK** is much different than attending networking events and meet-ups.

124 | Play Into Their Greed

The point is, ladies and gentlemen, that greed, for lack of a better world, is good. Greed is right, greed works. Greed clarifies, cuts through, and captures the essence of the evolutionary spirit. Greed, in all of its forms; greed for life, for money, for love, knowledge has marked the upward surge of mankind.

— Gordon Gekko (Michael Douglas)
Wall Street (1987)

Greed is good.

What do you think about **GREED**? When is greed good?

125 | Catch Your Dreams

Catch your dreams before they slip away
Dying all the time
Lose your dreams
And you will lose your mind

— *Ruby Tuesday* — The Rolling Stones
Keith Richards and Mick Jagger (1988)

If you don't have a dream, how can you have a dream come true?

— Jiminy Cricket

All our dreams can come true, if we have the courage to pursue them.

— Walt Disney

Hold on tight to your dreams — **ALL** of them.

Write down a dream that you let go of. Why did you let go? What is stopping you from pursuing it now?

126 | Protect Your Dreams

Hey. Don't ever let someone tell you, you can't do something. Not even me . . . All right? You got a dream you gotta protect it. People can't do something themselves, they want to tell you can't do it . . .

— Chris Gardner (Will Smith)
Pursuit of Happyness (2006)

Protect your dreams.

Think of a dream that you feel you cannot pursue right now. What can you do to keep it safe for later? What changes would have to happen in your life to make it possible?

127 | Give Them What They Want

I want ten chocolate chip cookies. Medium chips.
None too close to the outside.

— Howard Hughes (Leonardo DiCaprio)
The Aviator (2004)

It's that easy!

When was the last time you went out of
your way to give someone what he or she
wanted? How did you feel afterwards?

128 | Deliver the Girlfriend Experience

Chelsea: **Sometimes clients think they want the real you, but at the end of the day, they say they don't. They want what . . . they want what you want to be. They want you to be something else. They want you to be yourself.**

Interviewer: **Suppose I'm that rare client that really wants . . .**

Chelsea: **If they wanted you to be yourself, they wouldn't be paying you.**

> — Chelsea (Sasha Grey)
> *The Girlfriend Experience* (2009)

You can't always get what you want
You can't always get what you want
You can't always get what you want
But if you try sometimes you just might find
You get what you need

> — *You Can't Always Get What You Want*
> The Rolling Stones
> Mick Jagger and Keith Richards (1988)

Do I need to explain this to you?

What do you want? What do you need?

129 | Stay Away From the Boogeyman

Bart, I don't want to alarm you, but there may be a boogeyman or boogeymen in the house!

> — Homer Simpson
> *The Simpsons — $pringfield* (1993)

He's all in your mind; or is he?

I went to Sixty-Sixth Street School in South Central Los Angeles, back in the day when we could call it that. I rode my bike to school, and there was a tunnel under San Pedro Street that was supposed to safer than crossing the street. The big kids told the little kids that there was a boogeyman in the tunnel that would get them if they tried to get through it. I would tell kids that I would ride to the other side, exit out of the tunnel so they could see me, and then run back to them. I would tell them to give me their milk money (a nickel), explaining that they would lose it if the boogey man got me. But I promised them that, if I made it back, I would turn their nickel into a dime and give it to them. I gave away lots of dimes, but I had fun doing it.

**Give something valuable away.
Experience the pleasure fully.**

130 | Believe in Never-never Land

So come with me, where dreams are born, and time is never planned. Just think of happy things, and your heart will fly on wings, forever, in Never-never Land.

— J.M. Barrie
Peter Pan

It's okay I understand
This ain't no Never-never land

— *Centerfold* — J. Giles Band
Seth Justman (1980)

Ye'd best start believing in ghost stories, Miss Turner. Yer in one.

— Captain Barbosa (Geoffrey Rush)
Pirates of the Caribbean (2003)

Yes, Wendy, there is a Never-never Land.

Pick something impossible to believe in with all your heart. Make it real for you so that it can be real for the rest of the world.

131 | Never Brag

The first rule of The Fight Club is: you don't talk about Fight Club.

— Tyler Durden (Brad Pitt)
Fight Club (1999)

Never.

Look in a mirror and start bragging about something. Imagine that you are someone else listening to you and take note of how foolish you feel.

132 | Let Them Brag

I don't know how to put this, but I'm kind of a big deal. People know me. I'm very important.

— Ron Burgundy (Will Ferrell)
Anchorman: The Legend of Ron Burgundy (2004)

Stroke their egos. People love to talk about themselves; sometimes *ad nauseum*. One of the best things you can do as a Rainmaker is to get people to talk about themselves. When you let people talk about themselves, they feel like you care about them.

Go to a party or a bar and engage a stranger in conversation. See if you can get them to brag. Listen. Learn.

The silver lining to listening to people talk about themselves is not only the words you hear but the feelings that come with the words. Do you want to know how someone feels? Let them brag!

133 | Break Stuff

Move fast and break things. Unless you are breaking stuff, you are not moving fast enough.

— Mark Zuckerberg

And *keep* breaking it.

Pick three points in your home or office and move around the circuit as fast as you can, touching the wall at each location. Repeat as many times as necessary until you can cut your completion time by half. Everything can be done more quickly and efficiently! Rainmakers move.

134 | Find Their Achilles Heel

Ah, but remember, my friends. Even Tramp has his Achilles' heel.

— Boris
Lady and the Tramp (1955)

Everyone has one.

Watch the scene on YouTube, from *The Lady and The Tramp* (1955) when Lady and Tramp are sharing the same strand of spaghetti. What is Tramp's Achilles' Heel?

135 | Put Your Foot Down, Hard

Jean-Pierre Sarti: **Before you leave I want to tell you something. Not about the others, but about myself. I used to go to pieces. I'd see an accident like that and be so weak inside that I wanted to quit — stop the car and walk away. I could hardly make myself go past it. But I'm older now. When I see something really horrible, I put my foot down. Hard! Because I know that everyone else is lifting his.**

Louise Frederickson: **What a terrible way to win.**

Jean-Pierre Sarti: **No, there is no terrible way to win. There is only winning.**

> — Jean-Pierre Sarti (Yves Montand)
> Louise Frederickson (Eva Marie Saint)
> *Grand Prix* (1966)

Everyone else will be lifting theirs.

Watch this video on YouTube from *Grand Prix* (1966). Why does Jean-Pierre win?

136 | Don't Be a Social Media Whore

Dude this chick thinks she's the shit because @aplusk is following her on twitter . . . Yeah, she's just a social media whore.

— yiseowl
Urban Dictionary (December 03, 2009)

Social Media Whore (*Urban Dictionary*):

A person who has a psychological need to receive @replies and pings on Twitter, attention at tweetups, Facebook status update comments, and Facebook likes.

Rainmakers are not social media whores.

Regarding social media, I don't understand what appears to be the general population's lack of concern over privacy issues in publicizing their entire lives on the Internet for others to see to such an extent . . . but hey it's them, not me, so whatever.

— Axl Rose

Write down your time spent on social media each day for a week. Surprised?

137 | Choose Wisely

It is not our abilities that show what we truly are . . .
it is our choices.

— Dumbledore
Harry Potter and the Chamber of Secrets

The whole purpose of Starbucks is for people with
no decision-making ability whatsoever to make six
decisions just to buy one cup of coffee. So people
who don't know what the hell they're doing or who
on earth they are can, for only $2.95, get not just a
cup of coffee but an absolutely defining sense of
self: Tall. Decaf. Cappuccino.

— Joe Fox (Tom Hanks)
You've Got Mail (1998)

Order off the menu.

Do you make choices from your heart or
mind?

138 | Feel Outside the Box

It's fascinating that people, there's so many people now who will make judgments based on what you look like. I'm black. So I'm supposed to think a certain way. I'm supposed to have certain opinions. I don't do that. You create a box and put people in it and then make a lot of generalizations about them.

— Clarence Thomas

Don't put people in a box.

Think about how you feel about people.
Who do you put in a box, and why?

139 | Always Have an Opinion

So let us begin anew — remembering on both sides that civility is not a sign of weakness, and sincerity is always subject to proof. Let us never negotiate out of fear. But let us never fear to negotiate.

— John F. Kennedy
Inaugural Address (January 20, 1961)

You don't have to be right, or wrong, — just have one.

Write down your opinion on "Situational Ethics" as it relates to Rainmaking.

140 | Laugh

As you proceed through life, following your own path, birds will shit on you. Don't bother to brush it off. Having a comedic view of your situation gives you spiritual distance. Having a sense of humor saves you.

— Joseph Campbell
Reflections on the Art of Living:
A Joseph Campbell Companion

Have a comedic view of yourself.

Think about something that makes you laugh. How about a horse walking into a bar?

141 | Act From the Inside Out

As a result, the way we think, we act, the way we communicate is from the outside in, it's obvious. We go from the clearest thing to the fuzziest thing. But the inspired leaders and inspired organizations — regardless of size, regardless of their industry — all think, act and communicate from the inside out.

— Simon Sinek
How great leaders inspire action, — TEDTalks
(September 2009)

I have no formula for winning the race. Everyone runs in her own way, or in his own way. And where does the power come from, to see the race to its end? From within.

— Eric Liddell (Ian Charleson)
Chariots of Fire (1981)

Be a great Rainmaker. Act from your heart.

Think about a time when you over-thought something and missed an opportunity. What would have been different if you had followed your heart?

142 | Find Your Inner Peace

Peace. It does not mean to be in a place where there is no trouble, noise or hard work. It means to be in the midst of those things and still be calm in your heart.

— Lady Gaga

You see, she was gonna be an actress
And I was gonna learn to fly
She took off to find the footlights
And I took off for the sky

And here, she's acting happy
Inside her handsome home
And me, I'm flying in my taxi
Taking tips, and getting stoned

— *Taxi* — Harry Chapin
Harry Chapin (1972)

Peace is a wonderful feeling.

What brings you inner peace? Why don't you feel inner peace more often?

From OBITUARIES, The New York Times (by John Rockwell — July 17, 1981): "Harry Chapin, a folk-rock composer and performer active in many causes was hit from behind by a tractor-trailer on the Long Island Expressway in Jericho, L.I., the police said. He was 38 years old."

143 | Wear Black Socks

The player of the inner game comes to value the art of relaxed concentration above all other skills; he discovers a true basis for self-confidence; and he learns that the secret of winning any game lies in not trying too hard.

— W. Timothy Galloway
The Inner Game of Tennis

My father played tennis at UCLA. When he played against USC, he wore black dress socks with his traditional white tennis shirt, shorts, and shoes. His black socks distracted the players on the other side of the net affected their inner game.

Think about the last time you played the game by 'wearing black socks.'

144 | Distinguish Yourself

Be the one to stand out in the crowd.

— Joel Osteen
Your Best Life Now:
7 Steps to Living at Your Full Potential

Find a truly original idea. It is the only way I will ever distinguish myself.

— John Nash (Russell Crowe)
A Beautiful Mind (2001)

Stand out in the crowd.

My mother never told me "life is life a box of chocolates." What my mother told me from an early age was to distinguish myself from the crowd.

What makes you stand out in a crowd? How can you be a Rainmaker if you are invisible?

Part IV: Secrets

And now here is my secret, a very simple secret.
It is only with the heart that one sees rightly,
what is essential is invisible to the eye.

— Antoine de Saint-Exupéry
The Little Prince

Life Is Short — Very Short

Can you imagine us years from today?
Sharing a park bench quietly?
How terribly strange to be seventy

— Old Friends/Bookends — Simon & Garfunkel
Paul Simon (1968)

I have been listening to Simon & Garfunkel's song, Old Friends/Bookends, for almost 50 years; I turned 21 the month it came out. At 21, you think that you have all the time in the world. At 70, you know that time, not money, is your most precious commodity. There was a time in my life not that long ago when I could roll through my years in my mind and recall who I was with and what I was doing each year. Now, all the years are blended. Nothing describes the past better than Paul Simon's words from the song: "A time it was, and what a time it was. A time of innocence. A time of confidences."

Also on their Bookends album is *"Voices of Old People,"* a sound collage of taped audio recordings made by Art Garfunkel. *"Voices of Old People"* was shocking almost fifty years ago; now it is haunting to anyone who is a 'senior.' Getting old can be terrifying, carrying with it fears of illness, loneliness, and feelings of social obsolescence. Start taking care of yourself now, no matter how old you are. Discover love, health and happiness before it's too late.

Live in This World

In the Kingdom of Heaven, there is no grandeur to be won, inasmuch as there is an established hierarchy, the unknown is revealed, existence is infinite, there is no possibility of sacrifice, all is rest and joy. For this reason, bowed down by suffering and duties, beautiful in the midst of his misery, capable of loving in the face of afflictions and trials, man finds his greatness, his fullest measure, only in The Kingdom of This World.

— Alejo Carpentier
The Kingdom of this World

On the first day of their Hawaiian vacation Bob and Millie went to Hoku's brunch in Honolulu. Before Bob to could dig into the shrimp and lobster Millie took away his plate and gave him a plate of raw fruits and vegetables; reminding about his health problems.

Their plane crashed on the way home, and Bob and Millie found themselves at brunch in Heaven. Sadly, Bob started filling a plate with fruits and vegetables. An angel handed Bob a plate loaded with the same foods Bob had wanted at Hoku's. Millie glared at Bob and sneered. The angel told Millie: "Don't worry, he's in Heaven now." Then he told Bob: "You should have eaten what you wanted at Hoku's. It wouldn't have mattered."

Free Yourself of Your Hump

Do not free a camel of the burden of his hump; you may be freeing him of being a camel.

— G.K. Chesterton

G.K. Chesterton was an English writer. Per an article about his writing style in *Time* magazine on October 11, 1943: "**Whenever possible Chesterton made his points with popular sayings, proverbs, allegories** — first carefully turning them inside out."

Like G.K. Chesterton, I am going to take his quote and turn it inside out. "Free a camel of the burden of his hump and you will be freeing him of being a camel." Allegorically, we all have humps. Most of us carry our humps on our waists in the form of belly fat that is the result of toxins and stress.

Our mental and emotional humps are similar in that we cannot easily free ourselves from them. We can try to ignore them; we can try to mask our emotional pain with alcohol, drugs, or some other addiction such as sex or gambling. The only way that we rid ourselves of ourselves of our mental and emotional humps is to confront them and remove them through meditation and other techniques. Get rid of your hump; you'll enjoy being a racehorse instead of a camel. Unlike camels, we were not born with humps.

Enjoy the Bumpy Ride

Fasten your seatbelts. It's going to be a bumpy night.

> — Margo Channing (Bette Davis)
> *All About Eve* (1950)

Slash, who has described himself as being shy, has a great outlook on life: "Risk isn't a word in my vocabulary. It's my very existence." Onstage, Slash is far from shy; he is electric. He enjoys the bumpy ride.

Most of us have had very bumpy rides during our lifetimes. We have experienced lots of ups and downs. We have fallen to the ground, or have been pushed there, and have climbed to the top of the mountain, again and again. That's life.

Every time that happens to me, I try to enjoy the bumpy ride. Those bumps challenge us and keep us excited. A pilot flying straight and level often gets bored and climbs or dives or may change course several times during the flight. Although no one wants to fly into a storm, it happens: you have the choice enjoy the ride or not.

Betty Davis is often misquoted as having said: "Fasten your seatbelts. It's gonna be a bumpy ride." Whether it's just a ride, or the whole night, get ready. Life is a bumpy ride.

Make *Muchos Amigos*

If you really want to make a friend, go to someone's house and eat with him . . . the people who give you their food give you their heart.

— Cesar Chavez

The closing line from Casablanca (1942) comes from Humphrey Bogart when he turns to Claude Rains as they leave Morocco to join the Free French Army in West Africa: "Louis, I think this is the beginning of a beautiful friendship."

Friendship means different things to different people. Cesar Chavez believed " . . . people who give you their food give you their heart." I like that perspective of friendship as someone who gives you their heart.

Having real friendships in life is important. Real friendships are real friendships, not the kind that you make over greasy appetizers and watered-down drinks at some networking event where you are wearing a paper badge with your name scribbled on it with a black Sharpie and are there to pass out business cards. Real friendships are not ones where there is an underlying business angle. Real friendships are *real* friendships; based on mutual respect, admiration, and affection. Real friends are like Kevin and Winnie; like Peter and Wendy; like Forrest and Jenny; like peas and carrots.

203

Put a Smile on That Face

Why so serious?

— The Joker (Keith Ledger)
The Dark Knight (2008)

Almost everyone knows this line: "Why so serious? Let's put a smile on that face." from *The Dark Knight*. It sounds simple, and it reminds me of my 'horse walking into a bar' joke where the bartender asks the horse "Why the long face?"

This is the final secret, and it's very simple. Unfortunately, it's easier said than done. The next time that you're down when it's dark outside and darker inside your mind, look into a mirror and ask yourself: "Why so serious?" Then tell yourself: "Let's put a smile on that face."

It's just as easy — maybe easier — to smile than to frown. It's just as easy — maybe easier — to be happy than it is to be sad. Don't allow depression pull you down. Life is full of bumps. Fasten your seatbelt, put a smile on your face and enjoy your ride, bump-by-bump.

Wash Your Hands for Lunch

Fortunately, when our daughter Ali was growing up we could share many great experiences. When she was in kindergarten the teacher would scream "watch your hands for lunch" before lunch time. Ali and the other kids got excited and those words became an indicator that they were about to have fun — lots of fun!

Once we were riding down Pacific Coast Highway with some of her friends in our X5 and all the kids started yelling "wash your hands for lunch" out of the windows to people riding bikes and others on the sidewalk. They were having so much fun that it became addicting and I started yelling with them.

Ten years ago, our daughter, Ali, wrote me a note because she was concerned that I was unhappy with a consulting job that I had. Although I was making a lot of money I was working obscene hours in an emotionally toxic culture at a high expense to my health and happiness. This is what she wrote: "I remember daddy . . . I remember when he was super happy, you were so crazy and fun . . . remember yelling: 'Wash your hands for lunch'? Daddy be crazy!!! Daddy on the loose. Wash your hands for lunch!"

Yes, Ali, I remember. I love you.

Final Thoughts

May God bless and keep you always
May your wishes all come true
May you always do for others
And let others do for you
May you build a ladder to the stars
And climb on every rung
May you stay forever young
Forever young, forever young
May you stay forever young

— *Forever Young* — Bob Dylan
Bob Dylan (1973)

If you remember one part, and one part only, in this entire book, *this* is the one part to remember. Rainmaking is about making a positive impact on the world — on *your* world. You can choose to do it any way you want.

We often get lost in own private worlds and spin out of balance with the universe. That's what happened to Colonel Walter E. Kurtz — he left West Point dreaming of being a great soldier and ended up having nightmares of being a snail:

> [*intercepted radio message*] **I watched a snail crawl along the edge of a straight razor. That's my nightmare. Crawling, slithering, along the edge of a straight razor . . . and surviving.**

> — Colonel Walter E. Kurtz (Marlon Brando)
> *Apocalypse Now* (1979)

Writing this book has been a challenging experience for me, and an emotional one as I thought back on the 'Summer of 1969' when I left the beaches of my native California to discover America and work on Wall Street. That was the summer that Neil Armstrong walked on the Moon, Richard Nixon visited South Vietnam, the Manson Family scrawled "Death to Pigs" in blood during their Helter Skelter murder spree, and hippies and flower children were lured to the magic and music of Woodstock.

Woodstock was one of the defining events of the Sixties: it marked the end of one era and the beginning of another. The bullish Sixties, the "Go-Go Years," came screeching to a halt. We lost three of our heroes to assassins, and, more of our heroes — our brothers, fathers, and friends — never returned home from Southeast Asia.

We'd had enough of worrying about society and were hurling head-on toward the individualism of the Seventies when many of would exchange our idealistic dreams for society for materialistic ones for ourselves. We became, in the words of Don McLean, "A generation lost in space with no time left to start again." We had lost our innocence in villages like My Lai, in the mud of Woodstock, and in places like the Hog Farm and The Haight.

That summer, the one that Brian Adams sings about in *Summer of '69*, I carried with me a small paperback book: *The Mason Williams Reading Matter* — an eclectic collection of poems, essays, photos and short stories. I wrote on pages, turned down corners, and told his stories when I had a chance (especially the one about eating crackers in bed). That was a long time ago, but not so long as to forget the magic of Camelot and the belief that we *would* change the world. What I remember most about those years is my *feelings*. Like everyone else I was scared. Like most other people I was confused. And like the rest of the baby boomers I was passionate about my life.

My life has been shaped by feelings that were deeply implanted in me in the Sixties. More than anything else, I was influenced by John F. Kennedy's inaugural address, especially these words: "Together let us explore the stars, conquer the deserts, eradicate disease, tap the ocean depths and encourage the arts and commerce."

And I remember these thoughts from the same speech: What we do over our lifetimes determines the future of our planet. We have in our hands the power to develop ways to feed the world, transport ourselves, and provide the energy and infrastructure required to guarantee a better quality of life in the future; we also have, in those same hands, the power to destroy ourselves in minutes. Those who understand that have a responsibility to help create a newer world.

Your desire to make an impact on the world must come from within — it must come from your heart. It must be *your* dream. It must be *your* passion. Whatever it is, start working on it right *now*. Take massive and immediate action, commit, and don't look back.

Steve Jobs asked Pepsi executive John Sculley: "Do you want to sell sugar water for the rest of your life, or do you want to come with me and change the world?". In the words of Alfred, Lord Tennyson, from *Ulysses*: "Come, my friends. 'Tis not too late to seek a newer world."

In thinking back on the stories I heard from Wipala Wiki, I remember the role that storytelling has played in past civilizations. Storytelling has been the principal way that one generation passes along wisdom to future generations.

In modern times, storytelling remains the most powerful way to communicate emotionally. People love stories — especially ones that touch them emotionally. But, with that wonderful power of persuasion comes responsibility. I believe that, as Rainmakers, we have the responsibility to use the 'white magic' of storytelling and avoid the 'black magic' of storytelling.

Beyond everything else, don't take Rainmaking too seriously. Rainmaking is what we all do naturally every waking moment of every day. It's something we learned as infants and something we will be doing until we take our last breath.

We do best when we are doing what we love. Discover your passion and make following your dreams a priority every day.

Rainmaking morphed from a small book on selling into much more. We all have dreams somewhere in the stars. I have shared what's in my heart and mind knowing that, in some magical way, this book will impact you and what you do.

The concept for *Rainmaking* came from my wife, Alicia, who suggested that I create something different than the many books she has seen me browse and toss to the side. Between the lines of *Rainmaking* are some of the thoughts of my wife and our daughter, Ali. They've both impacted how I think and, more importantly, how I feel.

Throughout *Rainmaking*, I've leaned heavily on quotes, song lyrics and movies — not because I ran out of words, but because others said things better than I could have said them myself.

Over the months that I have been writing *Rainmaking*, Prince and Mohammad Ali died. Both made an impact on my life and the world. The lyrics of *Let's Go Crazy, Purple Rain, Little Red Corvette* and *Raspberry Beret* are playing on a continuous loop in my mind. The words of Mohammad Ali, especially "Float like a butterfly, sting like a bee," remind me of how self-belief, even to the point of cockiness, can drive someone to greatness.

Rainmaking: Impacting the World Through the Power of Emotions and the Magic of Storytelling is about influencing the world in a positive way. This book will help you make your personal impact on the world. That's not what I intended to do when I started writing this book, but that's what I believe will happen.

Where do you find that power? You know what I mean — the help you need when you have lost a sale or a deal. Or maybe the strength you need when you have lost a loved one. Have there been times when you have felt alone and disappointed? Of course, there have, and there have been times when you have felt that you have fallen so far down that you might never get up.

When that happens, when life seems dark and scary, that's when we seek to reach deep into our hearts and souls and search for some magical inner strength to help pull ourselves out of the abyss and back into the sunlight. Colonel Walter Kurtz was never able to escape the darkness and died because of it; as did Willie Loman.

And so, from where does that courage come? Where do we find the heart and passion that made Seabiscuit a champion? It comes from *within*. We all have it. Some of us can find it quickly; some of us must ask for help; but, we all have it.

Although Camelot is gone forever, I continue to hold on tight to my idealism and belief in the American Dream.

Thanks for investing your time to read my book.

Keep reaching for the stars. Always dance on the edge. Color outside the lines whenever you can. Wear black socks on the tennis court. And wash your hands for lunch.

God bless you, and may you stay forever young.

We didn't start the fire
It was always burning since the world's been turning
We didn't start the fire
But when we are gone
It will still burn on, and on, and on, and on . . .

— *We Didn't Start the Fire* — Billy Joel
Billy Joel (1989)

www.ingramcontent.com/pod-product-compliance
Lightning Source LLC
Chambersburg PA
CBHW070459200326
41519CB00013B/2641